COMMERCIAL PROPERTY INVESTING
EXPLAINED SIMPLY

COMMERCIAL PROPERTY INVESTING

EXPLAINED SIMPLY

STEVE PALISE

'*Commercial Property Investing Explained Simply* fills a gap in the market; with so many books for residential investors, at last a comprehensive guide to commercial property by an undisputed expert in this area'.

Adrian Butera – MD, Compton Green Real Estate and winner of the Real Estate of Victoria Auctioneering Championships 1999, 2001, 2004 and 2010.

'As somebody whose family has been around commercial property in Australia since 1956, Steve beautifully articulates the journey, but more importantly the OPPORTUNITY in diversifying your property portfolio, going commercial and elevating yourself to the next level.'

Andrew Morello – Winner of the first Australian *Apprentice* and Head of Business Development at The Entourage.

'After researching many industry professionals, I found Steve to be the most knowledgeable, sensible and sincere. He has now purchased over $3.2 million worth of commercial property for me across multiple states of Australia – and we are looking for our next one!'

Cameron Rowe – Sailor for Royal Australian Navy (age 30).

'Steve has helped many investors successfully invest in commercial property. Now he shares his expertise in this very readable, practical book.'

Grant Simpson – Founder of The Commercial Guys real estate agency.

First published in 2021 by Major Street Publishing Pty Ltd
E: info@majorstreet.com.au   W: majorstreet.com.au   M: +61 421 707 983

The moral rights of the author have been asserted.

A catalogue record for this book is available
from the National Library of Australia

ISBN: 978-0-6487964-1-1

Cover design by Tess McCabe
Internal design by Production Works
Printed in Australia by Ovato, an Accredited ISO AS/NZS 14001:2004
Environmental Management System Printer.

10 9 8 7 6 5 4 3 2 1

CONTENTS

WHY COMMERCIAL PROPERTY?

'Commitment unlocks the doors of imagination, allows vision,
and gives us the "right stuff" to turn our dreams into reality.'
— James Womack

In my work as a buyer's agent, whenever a client says they want to achieve a particular amount of passive income per year, I cheekily respond, 'And then what?'

A common first goal is to have $100,000 in passive income per year – and with commercial property, that's actually very achievable in a short period of time. But I find that people's answer to my question reveals the real driver behind their wealth creation. They usually want to spend more time with their children, to travel, to quit their job and work on something they're passionate about, or a combination of these.

So before you consider whether commercial property investing is right for you, it's important to decide what goals will make you happy. What motivates you? Assess your short-term, medium-term and long-term goals. I've spoken to thousands of people from different walks of life; some are over the moon when they can afford a new fishing reel, others when they can purchase a $250,000 sports car. Everyone's compass for happiness is different. Most people, however, overestimate what they need to achieve their happiness goals, and this means they take on unnecessary risk.

Be realistic with your goals, and don't just come up with a portfolio size or passive-income amount. Sacrificing time today for a specific number tomorrow may not be consistent with your personal values.

My own happiness comes from travelling, socialising, climbing mountains, feeling appreciated and working on passion projects. Property investing has enabled me to pursue these goals – I travelled, for example, to 30 countries by 30 years of age without sacrificing my professional career or my relationships. I'll never be someone with hundreds of properties in my portfolio, but I don't need to be, because my happiness doesn't depend on my numeric wealth – it's purely about choice and freedom.

My story

I'm now one of the most successful commercial buyer's agents in Australia, but I had humble beginnings in a gentrifying suburb of western Sydney. My father was a television repair technician, my mother was a stay-at-home mum and I have two older brothers (and even at 6 foot 3 inches tall, I'm by far the smallest of the bunch). We never felt poor, and were always cared for and looked after.

At high school, I finished in the top 1 per cent of the state, and at the time, thought academic excellence would equate to wealth – and that wealth would bring happiness. I had a natural affinity for mathematics and theoretical concepts that led me to study engineering at university, and I finished first in the course.

After university, life progressed well. I began to earn good money and became one of the youngest engineers in Australia to become chartered in both mechanical and structural engineering. My focal point has always been design, as in engineering it offers little room for subjectivity. It all comes down to the numbers! I had a vast array of design jobs, from designing medical equipment to designing mine sites.

Like many, though, I got caught up in the rat race. I was working long hours, earning a good salary and creating wealth, but I saw unqualified employees being promoted and earning high incomes while some of the most qualified employees were working hard but going unrewarded. My belief that academic excellence and hard work would be enough was shattered.

I decided that I didn't want my life as a professional to limit me, nor did I want to leave my financial future in the hands of a faceless corporate machine. So, I chose residential property as my path to financial independence. I spent countless hours reading every property-investing book I could get my hands on and speaking in depth with (and probably annoying) people in the industry who had 'made it'.

After three years of research, in 2012 I bought my first investment property in western Sydney for $230,000 – and saw it increase in value by $80,000 in one year. This was $20,000 more than my yearly salary at the time, and it was my light-bulb moment. I was hooked! Every year I purchased more properties, and my portfolio grew exponentially. Eventually, I bit the bullet, left my engineering career and went full-time into property. I became a buyer's agent and helped grow a buyer's agency into one of the largest in Australia.

Within a few years, I'd helped clients purchase more than 500 properties in the residential space. I was always fearful of commercial property though. Like everyone else, I'd heard that it was risky. I was told commercial properties did not achieve capital growth, had a high chance of vacancy and that, basically, commercial property investing was only for the wealthy. As I began to research, however, I quickly saw that it was all a misconception!

The returns on commercial property can be spectacular compared to residential property. And, as you'll see, you can mitigate almost all of the risk with thorough due diligence. For me, commercial property was the game changer, providing instant passive income and financial freedom.

The benefits of commercial property

Unless you plan to work your way up the corporate ladder to a very well-paid position, or to start a successful business or invent something, chances are you'll need to invest well to become wealthy.

I'm not trying to convince you that investing in commercial property is the best option for you, as investing in shares or residential property also has huge advantages if you know what you're doing. Still, in my view, commercial real estate can give you a financial freedom that other investments cannot.

However, if you're interested in shares or residential property, there are many blogs, magazines, newspapers and websites to keep you informed and make you a better-educated investor. There are very few resources for people interested in commercial real estate. I've now purchased hundreds of commercial properties for my clients, and have spoken with many accountants and mortgage brokers, and I constantly have to explain the benefits of commercial property and the misconceptions about it. This was what inspired me to write a summary of the key points to commercial investing, which after some intense labour, evolved into this book.

'Commercial property' can include any property that is held for the purpose of generating a return on investment. It comes in many forms, including industrial, retail and office, and some combination commercial and residential properties. All forms can be profitable investments, as you'll see. Long considered a more niche alternative to traditional investments, in recent years commercial real estate has started moving to the mainstream as a highly sought-after asset.

Some of the benefits of commercial property investing include:

- high cash flow returns
- stability of income
- low long-term risk
- exposure to different sectors of the economy
- tax benefits

- hedging against inflation
- investment control
- ability to add value
- leverage or financial gearing.

'Leveraging' is using debt rather than equity in one asset to buy another asset. This can allow you to make greater returns, but you can also lose more and end up in a negative position. People are scared of debt, yet even those who aren't wealthy take it on – for instance, in buying the family home. Leveraging to invest can seem scary, and there are lower-risk assets available, but commercial property offers a means to achieve big returns both in capital growth and cash flow, with minimal risk – if you know what you're doing.

It's imperative never to invest in something you don't understand – it's too risky, unless you seek reputable investment guidance. In this book, I'll educate you on the issues in commercial property investing and how to do it in a low-risk manner. I'll explain step by step how to analyse, select and buy commercial property, ensuring that the value of your investments will continually increase – so you end up making as much money as possible with as little risk as possible.

Note that I've written the book primarily for the Australian commercial property market, although many of the principles will apply worldwide.

Also, note that the strategies I outline here are designed for effective long-term investment. If you're looking for a get-rich-quick book on investing in commercial property, then this book probably isn't for you. However, if you want to understand how commercial property investing works and learn a tremendous amount of information you can apply, then read on! *Commercial Property Investing Explained Simply* will show you how to plan, find, analyse and build a profitable commercial property portfolio and avoid incorrect financial decisions. I hope you enjoy reading it and it opens your eyes!

PART I
RESIDENTIAL VERSUS COMMERCIAL PROPERTY

Property investors often debate whether to go residential or commercial. There are far more residential buyers than commercial, however, partly because those who favour residential property typically have little experience in commercial property. As everyone lives in some form of residential property, they feel they have a grasp of it, and it's considered a human necessity – although commercial properties do provide the resources and services necessary for our survival. There's also much more media coverage about people making money in the residential market, whereas commercial property is seldom spoken about.

About 70 per cent of residential property in Australia is owner-occupied, and so the owners have an emotional attachment to it. By comparison, commercial property is typically bought as an investment and purchased based on the numbers and return, even if it's going to be owner-occupied.

Most commercial purchases are valued based on their rental return. In the residential market, a property must increase in value for the buyer to make a profit, but commercial property can create wealth even without capital growth. A commercial property's rent is often also indexed to inflation, which means the market will rarely move away from you. In general, commercial net returns are much higher if you get it right, but can be riskier if you buy a bad property, as it could be vacant longer. If you buy a bad residential property in a good suburb, though, you'll generally be okay in the long term.

So, how can you decide whether commercial property investing is right for you? Let's look at some of the key differences between the two, in the table following. (Note that the figures given are indicative only – the exact numbers for a particular property will depend on factors like its location, type and versatility, and demand.)

	Residential property	Commercial property
Deposit required	10-20%	20-35%
Due diligence	Minimal	Comprehensive
Yields	3-6% gross average	5-8% net average
Leases	6-12 months	12 months - 30 years
Bonds	1 month	1-6 months and/or bank guarantee
Outgoings	Covered by owner	Covered by tenant
Repairs	Covered by owner	Covered by tenant
Depreciation	Average	Higher
Vacancy	1-2 weeks average	1 month - 2 years average
Cash flow	Negative to neutral	Highly cash flow positive
Loan interest rates	Variable over time	Generally 0.5-1% higher than residential
Capital growth	Market dependent	Market and rental increase dependent
Property management	Intensive	Low-medium effort
Value-adding	Renovations and developments (subdivision, townhouses, etc.)	More creative methods (ATMs, advertising space, etc.)

I'll go into detail about these differences in the relevant chapters later in this book, but here's a brief, general overview of each difference.

Deposits

For commercial property, you'll need a larger deposit than you do for residential. Lenders generally allow a loan to value ratio (LVR) of only 60 to 80 per cent for commercial property, whereas residential property lenders will allow LVRs of 80 to 90 per cent, or even 95 per cent. In other words, you'll need a 5 to 20 per cent deposit for a house or apartment, compared to a 20 to 40 per cent deposit for a commercial property.

So, the first perceived disadvantage of commercial property is that the cost to get into the market is high. However, in fact, the entry level for commercial property can be as low as $50,000 for something like a car park or regional office. Also, even in capital cities, industrial space can start at as little as $150,000. Another point that's often ignored is that the extra deposit required for commercial property is often recovered through cash flow alone within two years.

If your borrowing is dictated by the capital you hold, investing in commercial properties will mean you use less leverage, as they require a larger deposit and lower LVR. But if your main consideration is being able to service the loan, commercial property gives you finance options that residential does not. More on this in Part VI.

Due diligence

Once you've chosen the location for a residential purchase, the amount of due diligence required is quite small. It will typically involve a building inspection and a few checks on things such as whether the property is in a flood zone. If the area selected is of value, the property's worth will probably grow with the market.

Commercial properties, on the other hand, require an enormous amount of due diligence. You'll need to investigate and consider the asset type, the vacancy rate for that type of asset, the foot and road traffic around it, and conduct building inspections, a lease review, and a tenant review. Part V explains due diligence in detail.

Yields

Higher yields are the thing most often spoken about when it comes to commercial property. Residential property yields are gross yields, whereas commercial property yields are typically given as net yields. With residential property, the gross yields are typically between 3 and 6 per cent, and owning a residential property incurs considerable outgoings such as council rates, water rates, body corporate fees and maintenance. This can bring the net yield down to approximately 1 to 3 per cent after the outgoings.

Commercial properties, by comparison, will on average have a 5 to 8 per cent net yield. The reason it's referred to as a net yield is that the tenants will usually be responsible for 100 per cent of the outgoings. As you can see, with commercial property, you can receive a much greater multiplier of the net cash-flow return. This is one of the key reasons measured investors prefer to build a commercial property portfolio.

Chapter 6 has more information about yields.

Leases

There's a perception that commercial leases are more confusing than residential ones. In the past, this could be the case, as they were quite convoluted, but leases are now quite standard and much easier to read. Nonetheless, it's advisable to have a solicitor look over commercial leases, whereas with residential, it's enough for you and the property manager to check over leases.

Leases on both residential and commercial properties can be as little as month to month, however, residential leases are generally only 6 to 12 months, whereas commercial leases are from a year to 30 years long. In 1759, Arthur Guinness (founder of Guinness

Brewery) signed a lease on a brewery in Dublin for 9000 years! Residential tenants want the flexibility to be able to move should their circumstances change. Commercial tenants, by comparison, want the security of knowing they'll be able to remain at the location long term, as their business and livelihood depend on it. See Chapter 7 for more information.

Bonds

Residential properties usually have only a one-month bond, while commercial properties typically have a bond of one to six months. They can also have a bank guarantee for fulfilling the lease. A bank guarantee is a formal assurance by the tenant's bank that an amount of money will be paid to the landlord if the tenant does not fulfil their obligations under the lease agreement.

It's worth noting here that with residential property, the eviction process can take months and involves complicated legal proceedings. Evicting a commercial tenant is often much simpler with less red tape, as the property is not their home. More on bonds and guarantees in Chapter 7.

Outgoings

With residential properties, the owner is responsible for most costs, such as council and water rates, repairs and maintenance. With commercial property, the tenant is typically responsible for most if not all outgoings, which means a much higher cash-flow return for the owner. See Chapter 8 for further information.

Repairs

Residential tenants won't usually look after the property as if it were their own, which means more wear and tear and higher maintenance bills for the owner. Renovating a house can cost the owner tens of thousands of dollars, too – replacing old kitchens, bathrooms and carpet, for example, can get very expensive.

By comparison, in most cases, a commercial tenant is responsible for the property's internal fit-out and shopfront. The presentation of the property can be tied to their lease, too, so that the tenant is required to maintain it or risk breaching their lease and having it terminated. Commercial tenants will look after the premises generally though, because they've paid for the fit-out and pay the cost of maintenance. The condition and appearance of the property reflects on the business, meaning they're more likely to look after the premises in order to make a good impression on their customers.

They are also liable for the health and safety aspects of the property (staff and customer safety), and are likely to apply higher level of security features such as alarms, security guards and CCTV. The property will not be left unattended for a long period of time without your knowledge; whereas, for example, tenants of residential property may go overseas, leaving the property vacant and more vulnerable to intrusion, an uncontrolled fire and so on.

Depreciation

Unusually, for all real estate investment, including commercial, the depreciation is tax-deductible. No other asset class has this advantage. Depending on the age and style of the building, a commercial property will usually have higher depreciation due to the more expensive construction and fit-out, so this can be an advantage as higher depreciation means greater tax deductions for the owner. Chapter 9 goes into depreciation in more depth.

Vacancy

Vacancy rates are a significant point of difference between residential and commercial property. Residential properties in a well-chosen area will usually have a vacancy rate between one and four weeks per annum. There will generally be a higher turnover of tenants due to the shorter leases, as tenants may choose to move for work, because they've received a pay rise or lost their job, in order to buy a home or because their relationship status has changed.

Tenants of commercial properties, by contrast, are less likely to move because their livelihood is attached to the business, and they've paid for the fit-out. However, commercial properties in a high-demand region will typically have a vacancy rate of one to six months, and getting it wrong in commercial property can mean long periods of vacancy. With vacant properties, having the right marketing agent and the properties' rent priced correctly can assist in leasing the property more quickly.

Being able to afford the loan if your tenants move out is an important consideration here. Of course, this also applies to residential property, but with residential property, you will have shorter, more regular vacancies versus commercial, which will have longer vacancies less regularly.

People sometimes argue that commercial investment is riskier in terms of vacancy, but that's only true if you've bought a risky property – like buying the equivalent of a residential investment property in a mining town where rental demand is tied to the state of the resources sector. Even with a good commercial property, you still need a bigger cash buffer to cover aspects such as longer periods of vacancy, upgrades to the property or rental concessions (such as rent-free periods for tenant fit-out).

Cash flow

Most residential properties are negatively geared: you're losing cash flow in the hope that the capital growth will outweigh that loss. By buying this way, you might at some point have problems servicing the loan, and you'll also need to keep your job to be able to pay the mortgage. It is possible to find some good-quality neutrally geared or slightly cash-flow-positive residential properties, but even so, banks apply a serviceability criterion that will give your portfolio a negative cash flow in their eyes.

Commercial property has a high cash flow and servicing the loan is less of an issue, meaning that, as an investor, you can keep expanding your portfolio.

Take a look at these typical cash-flow examples for a residential property and a commercial property.

Residential property cash flow

Property: a house in the western suburbs of Sydney, bought for $780,000.

	Annual
Income	
Rent $500 p/w	$26,000
Expenses	
Loan interest (5% interest only, 80% loan)	$31,200
Council rates	$1,547
Water rates	$987
Building insurance	$1,200
Maintenance	$1,600
Property management	$1,400
Total	**$37,934**

For residential investment properties in Australia, the negative cash-flow position can be offset from the individual's income. If they're in the 37 per cent tax bracket, this would mean they get back $4,416 at tax time.

Pre-tax cash-flow position	-$11,934
Post-tax cash-flow position	-$7,518

Commercial property cash flow

Property: a warehouse in the western suburbs of Sydney, bought for $780,000 @ 7 per cent net yield.

Income	
Rent $1,050 p/w	$54,600
Expenses	
Loan interest (5% interest only, 70% loan)	$27,300
Total	**$27,300**

Ignoring the building, plant and equipment depreciation, and keeping the same 37 per cent tax bracket, the cash flow would be as follows:

Pre-tax cash flow	+$27,300
Post-tax cash flow	+$17,199

As you can see, the commercial property has a much higher cash flow for the same outlay as the residential property. It's worth noting again, however, that a higher deposit is required for a commercial property and this would affect the return on investment (ROI).

Chapter 11 contains more information and examples.

Loan interest rates

Commercial loans will generally have higher interest rates compared to residential loans. This will typically be around 0.5 to 1 per cent higher; however, this will completely depend on the type of loan, deposit amount, type of property and the risk. One of the reasons why commercial loans have a slightly higher interest rates is because they have a shorter loan term (e.g. amortised over 20 years instead of 30 years), which raises the monthly mortgage payments significantly. They also have a smaller secondary business market, so there is less competition between the lenders to provide a better rate.

In the last 20 years, interest rates have generally been under 10 per cent. Even though interest rates are much lower now, I have used an average of 5 per cent interest rates throughout this book for simplicity and conformity.

Capital growth

There's a myth that commercial properties don't grow in value at the same rate as residential. If this were the case, there would be a huge disparity in prices. It's just not true, though. Most commercial properties have shown at least the same growth as residential properties, though usually on a different cycle.

Residential property relies purely on capital growth to make a net return. In the property cash-flow example earlier, the house's value must grow at $7,518 a year just to break even. But the average capital growth rate of property in all capital cities in Australia over the past 30 years is about 5.3 per cent annually. For this property, this would equate to $41,440 capital growth in the first year and more each consecutive year due to compound growth.

Residential property is typically cyclical, with periods of high growth, low growth, no growth and even negative growth. A commercial property that is tenanted, by comparison, is more likely to have a steady income. The capital growth can also be cyclic, but it's of a different nature, which will be outlined in more detail in Chapter 12.

The growth in the price of most residential properties in Australia has meant that Australians' dreams of home ownership are slipping away as it becomes more unaffordable. For instance, in 1990, the median price of a house in Sydney was $194,000 and the average salary was $27,227. So at that time, the median house price was equivalent to 7.13 times the average salary. In 2019, by contrast, the median house price was $809,000 and the average salary was $65,500 – equating to a median house price of 12.35 times the average salary. It's arguable that residential prices in some regions may hit a ceiling due to unaffordability and the growth will slow, and so the historical growth of the past 30 years may not represent the future.

One point to note is that median household incomes have gone up because it's now much more common to have two working people in a household. This is one of the reasons most residential markets in Australia have grown so much.

As mentioned, residential property can have downturns, too, whereas commercial property with a solid tenant will typically remain at the same price or grow due to the annual increases in rent.

The perception is that there's a lack of growth in commercial property investment, but this is incorrect. If this were the case, you'd be able to buy in the commercial market much more cheaply than in the residential market. It's true that different commercial asset classes have different growth rates, but there's much more to it than that (read Chapter 12 for more). Investment in commercial properties is based more on mathematical algorithms than on market growth fundamentals. Residential property investment is based on the hope of growth.

Property management

Residential properties require considerable effort to manage, because the tenant is typically only responsible only for their electricity bill and council rates. The owner has to cover the cost of all other outgoings and maintenance. With commercial properties, the tenants are usually responsible for outgoings and maintenance, and so they require less work on the part of the owner. The tenants' livelihood depends on the property, too, as mentioned earlier, so they're more inclined to care for it. We'll look at property management in detail in Chapter 28.

Value-adding

Residential property investors often renovate, or buy larger blocks to then build granny flats or even subdivide the property. While these ventures can be profitable, that's usually the most value the investor can add.

Commercial property, as we'll discuss in Chapter 29, has the potential for many different kinds of development, according to the type of asset class purchased. The possibilities include changing the property's use; adding more tenancies; increasing the rent; creating new sources of revenue such as installing ATMs or solar power; or renting out parking, storage or advertising space; or adding mobile phone towers and repeaters. Commercial property is much more versatile.

***

You can see from this overview that commercial property has both advantages and disadvantages for investors compared to residential. With careful choice of property and location, commercial investing has the potential to provide a great return to the right investor.

In Part II, we'll look at the types of property you might consider purchasing and how to select properties which will fit your investing goals.

PART II
TYPES OF COMMERCIAL PROPERTY

Compared with the residential property market, commercial property can vary hugely. There are three main types of property – industrial, retail and office – plus some more niche types such as hotels, land and multi-family properties, and as an investor, you need to understand the unique characteristics and the risks associated with each type. Choose a single type to specialise in initially, so you can learn about it in detail and gain experience that will help you make profitable investments.

The Building Code of Australia divides properties into 10 classes, plus subclasses, if you're interested in getting an overall sense of all the types. You can find definitions here: www.qbcc.qld.gov.au/building-codes-australia-bca-classes-buildings.

Within the types, of course, individual properties can have a multitude of differences in terms of location, layout, type of building, frontage and foot and road traffic.

For investing and tenancy purposes, commercial properties are usually evaluated based on the building's age and location and the quality of the finishes. Different grading systems are available however the common classes internationally are:

- **Class A** buildings are the most desirable, featuring high-grade features and amenities and providing high status to their occupants.

- **Class B** buildings tend to be slightly older buildings that were once class A, but now lack some modern amenities and technological features. They usually lease for lower rents and are attractive to smaller tenants.

- **Class C** buildings are often older, slightly rundown and haven't kept up with the trends. Some can be refurbished to bring them back to class B or class A.

Banks take these classes into consideration when they're reviewing commercial property loan applications, and will lend on better terms for a class A property as opposed to a class C property.

We'll look at how to evaluate individual properties later in the book; for now, though, let's go over each of the broad types in turn.

CHAPTER ONE
INDUSTRIAL PROPERTY

Industrial property is a less glamorous class of commercial real estate, but historically it's a reliable performer. Most industrial properties are let on a net lease basis, which means the tenant pays some or all of the ongoing costs such as property taxes, rates, water, body corporate fees, building insurance and maintenance.

The increasing growth of e-commerce sales, a rise in business inventories, and faster deliveries are substantial drivers for industrial real estate.

Properties can vary in type from warehousing, factory, manufacturing to storage, and can vary greatly in size, from small warehouses to enormous manufacturing plants. They can have multiple tenants and often contain a mix of retail and office space as well, with the office space usually comprising 10 to 30 per cent of the total floor space for each tenant.

In terms of location, industrial properties can thrive in older or redeveloped urban areas if presentation is not important, but they need to be close to their service region and to population centres (in order to attract employees) and have good access to transport. Some locations specialise in particular types of industrial space or the area they service, and some types of properties, such as warehouses and distribution centres, are positioned for proximity to major highways or freeways. Being close to shipping locations, airports and so on can also be crucial, depending on the type of business which will lease the property.

For individual properties, a factor to consider is access to the building itself – roller door and internal roof height, access for trucks and space to manoeuvre them.

Fire protection is an important consideration, as most industrial properties can hold a large amount of inventory. The building's electrical capacity, floor thickness and load capacity, lay-down areas, ventilation, space for the disposal of dangerous goods and the potential for airborne by-products are other factors.

There also has to be enough onsite parking for staff and clients, and staff amenities like the kitchen, toilets and air conditioning in the offices are another important consideration.

The building's adaptability for future tenants also needs to be considered. Industrial buildings are usually very versatile for an array of types of tenants. Newer constructions are usually just three tilt-up concrete panels plus a garage door on the fourth side. Older designs tend to be brick construction.

To sum up, the key factors to consider when you're assessing industrial properties for investment are:

- location
- adequate access for large vehicles
- build type (iron construction, block construction or tilt-up concrete panels)
- generous roof heights to accommodate storage
- the building's suitability for various purposes in terms of electrical capacity, floor load capacity, ventilation and so on
- flexibility to include offices and showrooms

- sufficient onsite parking for staff and clients

- staff amenities.

Let's explore the three broad categories of industrial buildings – warehousing or distribution, manufacturing and storage – in more detail now.

Warehousing or distribution properties

Warehousing and distribution facilities are used primarily for the storage and distribution of goods and merchandise, and the main consideration is floor space. Usually less than 15 per cent of the total space will be devoted to offices, as floor space is a priority with less office staff. They require high ceilings to allow more cubic storage space and will typically have multiple roller doors to allow simultaneous loading and unloading. Some buildings will be specialised for cold or freezer storage.

Most developed countries now have less manufacturing than in previous years and more importation and warehousing, so they are designed and located differently than they used to be.

Generally, big multinational companies look for the following in warehouse and distribution properties:

- bigger buildings that have high ceiling space for more storage capacity

- buildings containing embedded technology to allow for automated operations or a higher office usage

- stronger and more durable concrete floors to accommodate taller pallet racking and heavier duty forklift trucks

- truck manoeuvring areas to accommodate trucks carrying containers.

This means that most older warehouse buildings won't suit their needs – but these are suitable for smaller businesses that have less turnover of product.

A flexible facility that can easily be reconfigured to accommodate a tenant's expansion or different requirements is a stronger and more versatile long-term investment. Flexible facilities will have multiple entries, large truck access and retail exposure, and their ratio of office to warehouse floor space will be adaptable.

Manufacturing properties

Manufacturing facilities are used for the fabrication or assembly of raw materials into products. Usually up to 20 per cent of the total space will be required for offices, as most manufacturing businesses have designers and more desk staff. Some premises have a combination of warehousing and manufacturing facilities, depending on the purpose of the business and its location.

Because low-cost manufacturing is surging in other countries, manufacturing can be high risk in commercial investing in Australia and other developed countries. The future of manufacturing is uncertain, as multinational firms balance their activities and interests with the growing movement towards protectionism. It's best to stick with manufacturing that requires a high level of quality control that's not available in low-cost countries. Some prime examples of this are medical products and food.

Because of this shift away from manufacturing, however, privately owned and publicly listed manufacturers are tending to sell their facilities – which are often older buildings sitting on huge, underused parcels of land. These are often redeveloped into housing or mixed-use industrial space.

Storage properties

Self-storage buildings – where a business rents storage space to other businesses and/or consumers – typically have several smaller tenancies and seem to be resistant to recession. Corporations are their biggest customers, using them for storage of hard-copy documents, general goods and oversupplied inventory.

The main types of storage building are as follows:

- **Outdoor bays or indoor storage bays** – simply a small warehouse with roll-up doors for vehicle access. These are the least expensive to rent.

- **Climate-controlled** – these are generally indoors and are typically used for more expensive items that are sensitive to temperature. A facility that has refrigeration can be used for cold food storage.

- **Specialty** – facilities designed to store particular items, such as cars and boats, documents, artworks, or wine or other alcohol.

- **Mixed-use** – these are storage buildings that can accommodate another business, perhaps with retail or office space, or by having laydown (temporary storage) areas or storage for car or truck rental, for example.

As storage facilities produce high yields, they are much in demand from investors, and management of them is relatively easy. The downside is that they're a low-cost proposition, meaning that it's easy for competitors to break into the market. Location is important – the facility needs to be close to its target consumer – but particular locations can become saturated, and when this happens, business can decline quickly. New competitors in the market can cause occupancy levels to drop severely, and these are critical to the business turning a profit.

CHAPTER TWO
RETAIL PROPERTY

Retail is typically defined as the sale of goods to the public in relatively small quantities for use or consumption, rather than for resale. It's quite common, especially in the past few years, to hear that retail spending is down; however, this generally refers to spending in large shopping centres owned by companies such as Westfield rather than in local shopping strips. Many types of retail properties are low risk, depending on their location and if they are an essential service.

Factors such as local demographics, median income levels, traffic volume, site configuration, residential and commercial density, and tenant mixes all play a part in the success of retail properties. Traffic needs to be suitable for the type of retail centre: small neighbourhood centres can thrive on secondary roads, whereas bigger ones require a primary arterial road.

Shops that are situated parallel to the road are generally superior to those that are perpendicular, as these have less street frontage and visibility. Signage should be easily visible for foot and road traffic and access in and out of the location should be easy.

For small retail centres, the leases are commonly on a net basis, which means the tenant pays some or all of the costs such as council and water rates, body corporate fees and maintenance. This generally suits the tenant, because the presentation of the business is paramount to its success and they would like to have responsibility for it. Larger retail centres, such as malls with lots of tenancies, will typically pay a flat rate plus a percentage of their annual sales. This means smaller businesses can afford to be in the centre, giving the property owner a good mix of tenancies that will bring more foot traffic.

It's worth mentioning that retail leases have specific legislation depending on the Australian state or territory they are in. Most retail shop leases are regulated by a retail leasing Act, and understanding the relevant Act is essential if you intend to lease premises to operate a retail business. Entering into a retail lease imposes additional obligations on the landlord. Commercial leases are governed by state-specific property and conveyancing laws.

Most of the retail Acts stipulate that certain particular costs cannot be passed on to the tenant. Some examples include:

- land tax
- expenses that don't benefit the premises
- contributions to a sinking fund for capital works
- management fees, unless the management fees relate to the management of the building or shopping centre in which the premises are located
- capital costs
- legal or other expenses relating to the negotiation, preparation or execution of the lease.

Let's take a look now at the main types of retail properties: medical, hospitality and service based, plus those for general retail.

Properties for medical businesses

Medical properties can be located in retail or office locations, depending on the target market. The medical sector has unique requirements such as additional plumbing and wiring to allow for medical room fit-outs, which makes the cost of construction and fit-out much higher than for a conventional retail space.

Specialist medical facilities will often be near a hospital, medical centre or pharmacy, and some will want street and consumer exposure to encourage business and will be a much more classical retail investment with high foot and/or road traffic. Office-based medical facilities, by contrast, are generally leased by specialist professionals who have appointment-based businesses.

These businesses have tended to be recession-proof, but be aware that this may change! Self-diagnosing equipment continues to advance, and a shift towards virtual assessment or 'telehealth' appointments may have been accelerated by the COVID-19 pandemic restrictions on in-person contact. However, at the moment these properties are usually very profitable and the tenants stable, with good long-term prospects. They have loyal customers and patients and service large areas.

Unlike ordinary retail properties, medical facilities can be in suburban areas and still be stable. The business owners will often do joint ventures, too, with other medical professionals such as pathologists in the same building, which makes them trustworthy from the banks' point of view as there are multiple stable businesses involved.

Properties for hospitality businesses

Food restaurants, particularly those with a takeaway service, are stable businesses and will always be popular. They will typically remain operating even with minimal profit. Depending on the location, however, the property may be subject to seasonal changes (such as holiday destinations). Some tourist areas and CBD locations have been hit hard during COVID-19, due to lack of international tourism, so this needs to be considered when selecting a location.

The fit-out costs are generally paid for by the restaurant rather than the owner, and as the costs tend to be high, operators will sell the business if possible rather than close down altogether – making the building a more stable investment. However, with some businesses, these fit-out costs will be absorbed by the owner through contributions in the lease, such as rent-free periods, rent reductions or shared fit-out costs.

Note that it's important to check the building insurance is covered and verified, though, as restaurants are a high fire risk.

Properties for service businesses

Everyone needs service businesses like hairdressers, barbers, nail salons, beauticians and massage centres; but, as an investor, it's wise to look for a business that has at least four skilled service staff. This ensures that the business can run without only one or two key people, and will also generally make it more profitable and stable in the long term. With four or more staff, the business is more likely to be sold than shut if the owner retires.

Service businesses can attract loyal customers, but need high foot traffic and affordable rent. A high rent without a proportionally high cost of service means a less profitable business for the tenant.

The cost of the fit-out needs to be assessed, as this can potentially determine how easily the business can move.

Properties for general retail

General retail covers a wide range of properties for businesses with different needs. Properties intended for lease to these businesses can be good investments, but here are a few to be wary of:

- **Supermarkets.** Large supermarkets are usually too expensive for the normal investor and have a low yield. Smaller supermarkets offer convenience, but most shoppers will go to large retailers for their major shop. Small supermarkets are needed to service areas where there's no big retailer.

- **Bakeries and butchers.** These were the stable businesses of the past 50 years, but there's been a slow shift away as consumers move to large supermarkets to do their shopping in one trip. Many bakeries are evolving to become a form of café. Beware of fad bakeries such as doughnut houses, which can get a big social-media following but then die out!

- **Newsagencies.** The newsagency is a dying business. Lottery tickets and newspapers used to be their bread and butter, but the value of both has diminished dramatically since they have become available online.

- **Specialty stores.** Bookshops, jewellers, discount stores, gift shops and hobby stores can be great or terrible. It's important to analyse any existing or potential tenant's business carefully to make sure it has long-term potential.

- **Childcare centres.** These can be in retail or residential areas, or even areas with office zonings. Childcare centres are very popular with investors, because they're seen as a necessity and usually have longer leases. However, many centres fail due to tight government restrictions on carer-to-child ratios.

CHAPTER THREE
OFFICE PROPERTY

Offices can often be confused with retail spaces – because they can, in fact, be interchangeable. All the retail properties outlined in Chapter 2 could be used for offices instead, or for offices combined with other uses. Typically, a commercial property is considered an office if more than 75 per cent of the interior is designed and finished as office space.

The reason offices are separated as a category of commercial property is that they usually require only a low-cost fit-out. Also, they're typically used as a base where people can work from, rather than being a place where goods are produced and sold.

Leases for office space are usually for three to five years, with tenants paying all outgoings. However, those in large buildings are usually leased on a gross basis, with the landlord being responsible for expenses. This depends on the location and style of property.

Office properties may be in a single-storey suburban building or in a high-density location, such as a city office tower. Note that Colliers, one of the largest commercial real estate companies in the world, classifies building heights as follows: low-rise – fewer than seven storeys; mid-rise – 7 to 25 storeys; high-rise – more than 25 storeys.

Entire office buildings tend to be bought by large syndicates and/or investment trusts, but smaller investors can buy office suites in a building for a much more affordable price.

An office space could be, for example, the operation centre for a big retailer, the premises for an accountancy or law firm, or the base for project management or a service business. Foot and road traffic are usually less important for office properties, as the types of businesses that lease them don't rely on foot traffic, especially if they're established. However, if the business is new or a franchise, being on the ground floor may be an advantage.

The geographical location of the office is critical, however it needs to be in a location where there are enough workers with the expertise the business requires.

The other important aspects to consider when evaluating an office are the aesthetics of the building and the internal fit-out, wheelchair and disabled access, the quality of the materials used, the availability of parking, access to public transport and roads and proximity to amenities. Many large office buildings now contain a café and have restaurants and shopping nearby which meet tenants' requirements. The building needs to be able to meet tenants' existing and future technology requirements as well.

The size and configuration of the floor plan are also important. Different tenants will require varying amounts of space, storage and warehousing, with the amount of space needed being determined by the type of work to be done there. A spacious office would have an average of 25 square metres per employee, including a proportion of the shared facilities, but this is sometimes reduced to 15 square metres per employee.

Changing demand

The most desirable tenants for offices are those with a good record in business or that are in a type of business that has the potential for growth – preferably in an industry that will be around for the long term. For numerous industries, floor space is becoming less important and the consideration of business type has never been so important.

The biggest influence on demand for office space is the job sector, which affects rental rate growth and the construction sector. Offices usually thrive when the economy is growing and companies are expanding. New industries can also increase demand and therefore growth. On the other hand, the office market struggles during flat and declining job growth.

Technology is playing a huge role in changes to offices. In recent times, it has become clear that physical space is becoming less important, with a shift to more flexible working arrangements and locations, and this has been accelerated due to the COVID-19 pandemic. This will occur not only in specific buildings, but in the design and mix of uses for larger-scale precincts. We are starting to see a growing demand for flexible work spaces and a shift towards higher-density workplaces to make property assets more efficient.

Overall, there's a shift away from the more traditional use of office space to more creative uses that allow for socialising and in-person idea exploration. This affects the fit-out and layout required to allow for co-working and open-plan designs.

With more employees working from home, too, some office areas are declining. The fact that residential real estate close to the CBD is so expensive means that workers are moving further out, enabling businesses to move to cheaper, smaller office locations.

With working from home becoming more accepted, it's likely that in the coming years, there'll be an increased focus on mental wellbeing and on integrating educational facilities within office environments to enrich the occupier experience. Office facilities will need to offer an enjoyable experience to get employees to attend.

CHAPTER FOUR
OTHER PROPERTY TYPES

Multi-family properties

The 'multi-family properties' category covers all types of residential real estate outside the single-family home, including blocks of apartments and boarding houses. Apartment blocks are split into multiple property subtypes (dissimilar to the commercial building height classification):

- **High-rise** – a building with nine or more floors and at least one lift. High-rise buildings usually have more than 100 apartments and are professionally managed.

- **Mid-rise** – a multi-storey building with a lift, and typically in an urban area.

- **Garden-style** – a one- to four-storey apartment building in a garden-like setting, whether in a suburban, rural or urban location. These usually don't have a lift.

- **Walk-up** – a four- to six-storey building without a lift.

- **Special-purpose housing** – a multi-family property of any style that targets a particular type of tenant, such as students or retirees, and subsidised housing.

Land

Land for commercial use comes in a range of types. The three most common are:

1. **Greenfield land** – undeveloped land such as a farm or pasture.

2. **Infill land** – this is land located in a city, which has usually been developed in the past but is now vacant.

3. **Brownfield land** – a parcel of land previously used for industrial, mining or commercial purposes that's now available for re-use. These properties are generally environmentally impaired and require rectification for habitable use.

Hotels

The hotel sector provides accommodation to travellers and tourists. Hotels can be independently run or part of a chain. They're usually split into four categories:

1. **Full-service hotels** – which are usually located in central business districts or tourist locations, and are generally part of a big chain such as Four Seasons, Marriott or Hilton.

2. **Limited service and boutique hotels** – these are usually smaller and don't normally provide amenities like room service, onsite restaurants or convention space.

3. **Extended-stay hotels** – designed for stays of a week or more. They have larger rooms, small functional kitchens, and are designed for guests to be self-sufficient.

4. **Resorts** – full-service hotels on a large land area. They're typically in lifestyle location where occupants will come for rest and recreation, and have amenities such as golf courses, outdoor swimming pools and activity services for children.

Buying an entire hotel should be approached with caution, as it's more like running a business than having a passive property investment. As the hotel business is generally high risk, it can be difficult to raise funds to build a hotel project. Hotel developers will sometimes sell individual apartments under a strata title, however, to raise funds for the project. Some operators will offer fixed leases to the buyers, while some offer a share of the income generated by that unit from the hotel operation.

Serviced apartments within a hotel complex generally offer a high guaranteed rental return. They usually promise security, as they typically involve a leaseback agreement with the hotel operator, and these guarantees usually expire after one to five years. After that, the returns can drop significantly if the hotel does not maintain a low vacancy rate. Finance for serviced apartments is often hard to obtain due to their high-risk nature. Also, with more and more serviced apartments available, oversupply may hinder the category's capital growth.

Special purpose

There are plenty of other types of commercial real estate beyond the major categories mentioned thus far. Special-purpose commercial real estate includes things like activity centres for indoor sports, petrol stations, car washes, theme parks, marinas, movie theatres, funeral homes, community halls and churches. These can be profitable investments; however, it's crucial to understand the market and niche they are in.

Leasehold property

Freehold property is the most common form of property, where you own the property outright – you own the land and all non-moveable inclusions such as the building for an indefinite time, and can make changes as you please as long as they're within council regulations.

Being a freeholder allows you to lease the property to others for as long as you want, at your discretion.

In contrast, leasehold property, as the name suggests, is a lease on property owned by the Crown (the state). With this type you 'own' the land and property for only a set time, and changes to the land and property are subject to local government legislation and must be approved by the owner (the Crown).

Leasehold titles are not as common as freehold titles, but are common in Australian rural areas where the Crown owns the land under pastoral leasehold. Both the length of the lease and the type of activity that can be undertaken on the land are restricted. All land in the Australian Capital Territory (ACT) is leasehold.

It is possible for leasehold property to be converted to freehold: some Australian states or territories will allow this and permit the leaseholder to pay for the land in rent instalments. The property becomes a freehold when the last instalment is paid.

These Crown lands should not be confused with other types of Crown or state-owned lands, such as national parks, state forests, state rail property and other government-owned infrastructure.

PART III
THE NUMBERS

Commercial property investment is all about the numbers. It's important to use objective measurements to determine whether a property is worth buying, so in this part of the book, we'll look at the numbers you should analyse when you're considering an investment purchase:

- the purchasing costs
- the yields
- leases
- outgoings
- depreciation
- the capitalisation rate and property value
- cash flow
- capital growth.

In the last chapter of the section, we'll explore growing your portfolio.

CHAPTER FIVE

PURCHASING COSTS

Commercial properties have the same purchasing costs as residential property, but with a couple of additions. A rough estimate used in the industry is that buying costs outside of your deposit will equate to about 5 per cent of the purchase price. In terms of deposits, some lenders offer 65 per cent, 70 per cent or 80 per cent loan to value ratio – so you'd need a deposit of between 20 and 35 per cent. Once you've spoken with a commercial broker or lender and know the deposit required, you can work out your purchase price budget.

A simple way to this is to divide your available deposit by the lender's deposit requirements and add 5 per cent to cover items such as legal costs, inspections, valuations and government taxes. Your available deposit should not include your buffer for leftover savings.

For example, say you have $150,000 to spend and the lender requires a 30 per cent deposit. You also need to allow 5 per cent for purchasing costs, bringing the total up to 35 per cent. If $150,000 represents 35 per cent of the total, the maximum you can spend to buy a property will be $428,571. So, you should be looking at properties that cost less than $425,000. Typical purchasing costs are:

- stamp duty
- goods and services tax (GST)

- legal/conveyancing fees
- the cost of valuation for lending approval
- body corporate inspection report
- the cost of a building inspection
- the cost of a pest inspection
- the cost of a survey.

I recommend you obtain quotes on all services before proceeding with the purchase, as well as seeking advice from a property-investment-savvy, tax-qualified accountant.

Let's look at each of these now.

Stamp duty

Stamp duty is a government tax on certain transactions – generally applied when you buy a motor vehicle, an insurance policy or real estate. Stamp duty on a property can also be known as 'land transfer duty'. The amount of the duty varies depending on the Australian state or territory the property is in and the purchase price.

Goods and services tax

The sale of a commercial premises can attract goods and services tax (GST). This is currently 10 per cent of the purchase price, so it's a significant addition to the purchase. GST is generally imposed when a seller is registered or required to be registered for GST and is conducting an enterprise. If you, as the buyer, are registered for GST, it can be claimed back in your next business activity statement, but the money still has to be paid upfront to the seller.

There are exemptions to the application of GST, however. For example, a seller doesn't need to apply GST if the property is part of a 'going concern', which usually means there is an ongoing business operating after settlement. Leasing a property is deemed a business and therefore a going concern. In order to avoid GST, the buyer must be registered for GST or be required to be registered. It's important to seek independent legal and financial advice to ensure you won't have to pay GST. If the property is not sold as a going concern, GST will be payable, but if the buyer is registered for GST, they can claim the GST back.

The property will be considered a 'going concern' if:

- the sale includes everything that's necessary for the continued operation of the current business

- the business is carried on by the buyer until the day of sale and continues after the day of sale.

Most tenanted properties are bought as a going concern and so GST in most instances is not applicable. You may need to allow for GST for untenanted properties, though.

Legal or conveyancing fees

Legal or conveyancing fees are paid to your solicitor, and include the solicitor's fees and the costs of the searches they need to undertake for your purchase. A solicitor's charges for a purchase will usually range from $1,800 to $4,000 depending on the value of the property being purchased and the amount of leases.

Valuation costs

Valuation costs are incurred when you obtain finance from a lender. Lenders will only accept valuers who are on the list they've drawn up. Charges will typically be from $800 to $3,000 per commercial property purchase, though they'll be higher if the property has multiple tenants.

Body corporate inspection report

If you're buying in a strata property, it's important to get a physical body corporate inspection report. This will identify any issues with the specific lot or common property. It will also notify you of any planned special levies to be imposed after settlement.

Building inspections

You will also pay to have a building inspector analyse the property and detect any defects. An external inspector who hasn't been recommended by the selling agent is preferable, as they'll be unbiased. I recommend using an inspector who takes a lot of photos and provides descriptions of each item as opposed to using tick-box forms. Building inspections typically cost $350 to $800. If the building inspector is qualified for pest inspections, this is usually performed at the same time.

Pest inspections

You'll need a pest inspection, as you would for a residential property purchase. You may be able to engage a building inspector who's also qualified to perform pest inspections. Pest inspections typically cost $200 to $500.

Surveying

If no survey is supplied with the contract of sale, it's wise to have one done. Your solicitor or the selling agent should be able to give you a list of surveyors in the area.

Other fees

In addition to the fees already mentioned, there are usually some small miscellaneous fees such as registration and bank fees.

CHAPTER SIX
YIELDS

A commercial yield is expressed as a percentage – the annual rental income the owner receives from the tenant or tenants compared with the purchase price. There's a lot of conjecture about whether a commercial yield should be calculated based on the gross or net, so let's clear that up: while residential yields are gross yields, commercial yields are typically given as net yields. In other words, they are calculated based on the property's net income rather than its gross income:

- **Gross income** is the total income collected from the property. It includes rent and any other extras such as payment for electricity, water, rates, property management and other outgoings, if the tenant is paying these.

- **Net income** is gross rental income less all expenses such as council rates, water rates, insurances, maintenance and property-management expenses. It's the amount the owner receives after all expenses have been paid. This excludes your mortgage repayments, however.

Put simply, a commercial yield is the net income divided by the property value, and represented as a percentage. Here's an example.

Yield calculation

Property purchase price: $500,000
Gross income: $43,000
Outgoings: $7,000 (paid by owner)
Net rent: $36,000
Property yield: $36,000 ÷ $500,000 = 7.2%

You can do this calculation in reverse to obtain a purchase price that will give you the yield you'd like:

Purchase price calculation

Desired yield: 7.2%
Gross income: $43,000
Outgoings: $7,000 (paid by owner)
Net rent: $36,000
Purchase price: $36,000 ÷ 7.2% = $500,000

CHAPTER SEVEN

LEASES

A lease is an agreement that allows the use of a premises or building by a tenant to conduct their business, in return for the payment of rent to the owner of those premises. The lease will usually begin when both parties sign it. Once the lease is signed, the landlord and tenant usually can't end it without the other party's consent, or a break clause will apply and a penalty amount will become due. So, when you buy a leased commercial property, you're buying a guaranteed income for the term defined.

A lease benefits both the tenant and the owner: the owner is happy to have a reliable source of rent for an extended period, and the tenant is happy to have the security of a long-term location where they can expand their business. If one party wants to part ways, however, the situation can become difficult.

In multi-tenancy commercial properties, tenants may complain about such things as the temperature in the building at certain times of the day, the cleaners not doing an adequate job, noisy neighbours or mould dangers. They may use these points to claim the owner is not holding up their part of the lease and look for a rent reduction or penalty-free early exit.

Clear and well-worded leases can avoid the expense and stress of potential disagreements. The lease sets out all conditions between the lessee (tenant) and the lessor (landlord), clarifies the relationship between the two parties and ensures the expectations of both are clearly understood and documented. It includes the terms and conditions of the tenancy, including how you, as the owner, are to be paid, when rent increases will take place and how they'll be calculated.

The lease process

With the help of a solicitor, drawing up a lease is usually a straightforward process, although there may be quite a bit of back and forth negotiation over the lease terms. There are four steps:

1. **Creation and signing of an 'agreement to lease' document.**
   This is prepared before the formal lease is drawn up. The agreement to lease is an agreement to grant a lease in the future, without actually granting a right of possession to the proposed lessee. It can be used if the lessor has not acquired title to the land yet, the premises have not been fully erected or made ready for occupation, the former tenant is still in occupation of the premises, or all the lease conditions have not been fully settled. The agreement to lease is not a legally binding document.

2. **Submission of a draft lease by the landlord (the lessor).**
   Their solicitor will prepare a lease based on the criteria outlined in the agreement to lease document. The lease is then sent to the tenant, whose solicitor will review it and may ask for changes. The lessor's disclosure statement is also submitted. A disclosure statement is a document that must be provided by the seller or landlord which sets out prescribed information about the property, such as detail of mortgages, covenants, easements, zoning and outgoings. Registrations and survey costs are incurred at the expense of the tenant.

3. **Finalisation of the lease.** Once agreement has been reached between both parties, three copies of the lease are provided to the tenant's solicitor by the landlord's solicitor. The tenant will then sign all copies, return them to the landlord for signing, and receive one copy back for their records. Security bonds and guarantees (which we'll discuss in the next section) are also provided at this stage.

4. **Registration of the lease.** Typically, if the lease period exceeds three years, including any renewal options, a memorandum of the lease will be prepared and registered with the Land Registry Services.

Lease inclusions

The following information is mandatory in every lease:

- tenant details
- description of premises and use
- guarantor details
- bond details
- start and end date of the lease
- the length of the lease
- options on the lease
- how much the rent is
- details about rental increases and reviews
- details of any outgoings the tenant must pay
- who has responsibility for repairs and maintenance – usually these are covered by the tenant
- the core trading hours and when the premises will be open for business
- any additional factors such as fit-out or rent-free periods
- insurance.

It's not essential, as a buyer, to understand every detail of the lease, as your solicitor will be an expert in contractual law and will review all the proposed terms and conditions. It is important, though, to be familiar with all the lease terms, to enable you to secure a better property and negotiate well.

Almost everything is negotiable in a commercial lease. As the landlord, your main focus should always be on ensuring that your property is a solid investment with a good long-term tenant.

Types of lease

There are four main types of lease for commercial property: gross leases, net leases, triple net leases and absolute net leases.

Gross leases

A gross lease is full service – the property owner pays for all the outgoings, and the tenant is responsible only for the rent. As the owner, with a gross lease you incur the risk that outgoings such as council and water rates or insurance premiums may increase. Since you can't raise the tenant's rent until it's due for review, this can affect your yield, making your initial calculations on the profitability of the property inaccurate.

Net leases

A net lease generally means the tenant pays for one or more of the property's outgoings in addition to their rent, such as the council rates or maintenance costs. The owner is generally responsible for property management and land tax, but they must supply a disclosure statement to the tenant outlining which outgoings the tenant is responsible for.

If the property is multi-tenanted, each tenant will need to cover their portion of the outgoings as agreed in the lease.

The benefit of a net lease for you, as the owner, is that the tenant will pay any increases in outgoings, so your cash-flow calculations will remain accurate.

Triple net leases

In a triple net lease, the owner is responsible for the structure, roof and parking area, while the tenant is responsible for all other expenses.

Absolute net leases

With absolute net leases, the tenant is responsible for absolutely everything relating to the property – the rent, plus all rates, taxes, insurances, management fees, the structure, repairs and maintenance.

Lease periods

Leases can be for any period, but most small to medium businesses will have between a one- and five-year term. For startups, it's more likely to be one to two years, because the tenant isn't keen to commit to a longer term. Leases for well-established businesses may go for three to five years. For national chain tenants such as big shopping centres, hardware stores, petrol stations and established fast-food outlets, leases are typically seven to twenty years.

Generally, though, leases are for three, five or ten years, and they typically have multiple terms and options to renew: for example, '3+3+3', meaning three periods of three years. At the end of each term, the tenant has the option to renew.

The pros and cons of different lease periods

Lenders will look closely at the length of the lease when agreeing to finance your purchase of the property; a newly signed lease or a longer lease can drastically increase the value of a property and your lender's willingness to finance you. Short leases, by comparison, can be a risk or an opportunity. The risk is that the tenant might not stay; the opportunity is that at renewal time, they may sign a long lease. Also, if the tenant has been paying a lower rent, the renewal is an opportunity for the owner to increase it.

If the location is right but the tenant is wrong, even if that tenant doesn't renew, the next tenant could be better. You'll need to check vacancy rates especially carefully with this strategy, however.

From the tenant's point of view, the length of the lease is a big part of the value of their business, as a long lease secures their location for the future. The length of the lease is especially important for some businesses such as shops and industrial enterprises, for which foot and road traffic are critical and the fit-out may be expensive.

In some instances, when the tenant is looking to sell their business, they'll request more lease options to attract a sale. This is a win-win for the tenant and the landlord. If the business owner wants to sell out during the period of the lease, they may need to guarantee a new tenant for the balance of the lease.

Having a long lease can also save money on solicitors' fees, as the tenant can simply exercise their option to extend the lease term rather than you having the solicitor draft a new lease. As an investor, though, you want the lease to state that the tenant must exercise their option to extend it at least six months before the lease expires, to give you time to advertise if they don't renew. The prospective renewal should begin to be considered about 12 months before the lease expires.

On the negative side, if your investment is a small shopping centre, with long leases you don't have any flexibility to change the tenants or mix of shops until the leases are complete. Also, if a tenant is on a long lease and the zoning of the area changes, you could have difficulty redeveloping the site.

Lease period negotiations

The terms and options in the 'agreement to lease' and then the lease are usually the starting point of a negotiation between the landlord and tenant. A startup or tenant with a newer business will want shorter terms plus lots of options to renew; the landlord will try to negotiate longer terms with options because this adds value to the property. It can be worth considering shorter initial terms to achieve a slightly higher rent, however.

When negotiating, it's essential that you know the local market and comparable properties and what they're being rented for. It's important to inform the tenant about what other lease terms are being used on similar premises to assist with realistic expectations.

Renewing a lease

If the tenant wants to renew the lease, the owner typically has two months to dispute the request. If, as the owner, you grant the request, you can negotiate new terms at this point. You'll need to get an independent valuation to determine a new rental fee, if applicable.

If it is a secured lease (with bonds and guarantees), the tenant has the right to remain in the property under the terms of the existing lease while the new terms are negotiated. If it's unsecured, the tenant has no right of occupation after the end date of the existing lease, and the owner can demand they vacate immediately.

In some states of Australia, if there are no options left on the lease, legislation requires the owner to give priority to current tenants over new tenants. However, in most states, this isn't required, and whether or not a new lease is signed depends on negotiation between the tenant and owner.

Vacating or ending a lease early

If the tenant is vacating at the end of the lease period, they must leave the property clean, tidy and in original condition, without any damage. Depending on who owns the fit-out, they may be responsible for its removal. The terms of the lease will determine what is required.

If the tenant wishes to exit the lease early, it is possible for the property manager to market the property and have the current tenant wear the costs (if reasonable) for marketing, incentives and leasing. The advantage to the owner is they're able to be finicky about who the new tenant may be, as they'll still be receiving rent from the current tenant.

It's possible for an owner to end a lease early if the premises require significant reconstruction, repair or renovation (particularly if the property is uninhabitable). In this case, the owner must give the tenant adequate information about why the property needs significant work.

Assignment of leases

One of the great advantages of commercial property is that, as mentioned earlier, if your tenant sells their business, they'll probably have to guarantee that the new business owner will continue to pay the rent. If the new business struggles and the rent goes unpaid, the previous tenant's guarantee is still valid. Leases are legally binding; assigning the lease to a new tenant protects your interest, as the landlord. For instance, it stops a tenant selling their business for a small amount and walking away from their responsibility.

If your tenant is selling their business, it's imperative that your solicitor handles the process of assigning the lease to the new business owner.

Security bonds and guarantees

Landlords of commercial properties usually require some form of security from the tenant to protect themselves in case the tenant defaults under the lease. Security bonds and guarantees provide monetary assurance that the tenant will uphold the conditions of the lease. Usually, a tenant pays between one and six months' rent as a cash deposit/bond.

In addition, tenants can supply a bank guarantee, personal guarantee, a parent-company guarantee or a cash deposit. Let's go over the basics about these types of security now. It's preferable to have both a bond and guarantee when assigning a lease.

Cash deposit/bond

A cash deposit or bond is an amount of money provided by the tenant, usually by way of bank cheque at the commencement of the lease. The bond is generally transferred to the new owner if the property is sold. Depending on what state or territory the property is in, you may be required to have the cash bond held by a government entity. If not, the cash bond is usually paid into the owner's bank account or into the property manager's trust account. Most investors will prefer to have the bond in their personal account, as it enables them to, for example, put the funds in a high-interest saving account. When the lease ends, you'll be obligated to return the cash bond to the tenant, together with interest (if stipulated by the government entity or in the lease).

The main advantage of accepting a cash bond is that it's easy to collect and means the tenant doesn't have to deal with a banking institution, which can delay security being provided.

Bank guarantee

A bank guarantee is a formal assurance by the tenant's bank that an amount of money will be paid to the landlord if the tenant does not fulfil their obligations under the commercial lease agreement. Landlords generally prefer bank guarantees, for several reasons:

- They're provided by a third party.

- The bank is required to honour any drawdown request without first checking with the tenant.

- Bank guarantees survive the tenant's insolvency, which reduces the risk to the property owner.

The bank requires the tenant to pay a cash deposit, secure the lease by a mortgage or other asset, or provide another minimum-balance facility, which ties up the tenant's funds and usually costs a premium to maintain.

Many banks require the bank guarantee to have an expiry date, so it's always worth checking this. In addition, if you buy a property where bank guarantees are already in place, it's essential to go through the process of having these re-drawn in your favour. The issuing bank is unlikely to accept that you're entitled to the guarantee funds simply on the basis that you are now the landlord. It is essential that a solicitor be used for this transfer.

Personal guarantee

A personal guarantee is an assurance from the directors and/or shareholders of the tenant's business that the tenant will fulfil the obligations of the lease. In the event of a default, personal guarantees require the guarantors to pay the defaulted amount out of their personal funds or assets.

However, a personal guarantee is only as valuable as the individual giving the guarantee. If they don't own any assets of value, the guarantee may not be worth much. Please note, there are no statutory demands in relation to personal guarantees. You may need to commence proceedings to recover the funds from the guarantor.

Parent-company guarantee

A parent-company guarantee can apply if the tenant entity is a subsidiary of a parent or holding company – for example, a franchisee obtaining a guarantee from the franchisor. This may be preferable to a personal guarantee, but it's worth noting that parent companies, even those listed on the stock exchange, can become insolvent. Be extra cautious if the parent company is a foreign entity, as enforcement can be expensive. Enforcing a corporate guarantee is usually easier than enforcing a personal guarantee, however, as in a lot of circumstances, the landlord can issue a 21-day statutory demand. Beware though: at the time of writing the 21-day period had been temporarily extended to six months because of the COVID-19 pandemic.

Fit-out

The lease will include clauses specifying the criteria for the initial fit-out of the premises, and also for what's required at the end of the lease. Fit-outs can be expensive both to install and to remove to return the property to its original state, so fit-out guides are often included with the disclosure statement to ensure both parties agree on what's required and expected.

The quality of a fit-out is often a contention between the tenant and the landlord, especially if it will directly affect the value of the property. In some instances, the landlord will buy the fit-out from the tenant if they are exiting the premises. The fit-out could be owned by the tenant or the owner, and this agreement should be as detailed as possible to avoid disputes.

Rent increases

Most rental increases for each year of the lease will be the same as the Consumer Price Index (CPI) or 2 to 5 per cent. At the end of the lease term, the rent can be negotiated to bring into line with the market. With shorter leases, this is not as significant, but with longer leases (10 to 20 years), it's critical that the rent reflects what the market is doing. Beware, though, because some leases have caps on market increases during the option periods.

At the time of lease renewal, the amount will usually default to a 'market review', when the landlord will look at comparable rents. Once the landlord has the latest figures, the tenant can decide whether to accept, renegotiate or not renew the lease.

Note that it's best for both parties that the rent goes up evenly and regularly rather than there being a big increase in a market rent review farther down the track. Some buyers will want big increases such as 5 per cent each year, but this can aggravate the tenant if the rent climbs above the fair market rate and they can't renegotiate it until they extend or renew their lease.

It's important to review the rents of your properties at the end of their lease terms as this will have a large impact on your cash flow. An increase needs to benefit both the tenant and owner, as they ultimately drive the success of the investment. If the tenant isn't succeeding or adding to your commercial investment, it may be best to find a new tenant.

Three common methods for reviewing and increasing rent are:

1. Consumer Price Index

2. fixed increases

3. market review.

Consumer Price Index method

The CPI provides a general measure of inflation for all Australian households. It measures only the changes in prices that private households face.

The simplest way of thinking about the CPI is to imagine a basket of goods and services comprising items bought by Australian households. As prices change from one quarter to the next, so too will the total price of the basket. The CPI is simply a measure of the changes in the price of this fixed basket of items. The total basket is divided into 11 major groups, representing a specific set of commodities:

1. food and non-alcoholic beverages

2. alcohol and tobacco

3. clothing and footwear

4. housing

5. furnishings, household equipment and services

6. health

7. transport

8. communication

9. recreation and culture

10. education

11. insurance and financial services.

CPI is an important economic indicator and is used when the Reserve Bank formulates monetary policy. It's the accepted standard for rental increases on commercial leases in Australia. The market and demand for the property are also considered; however, CPI is the most accurate method for long-term forecasting.

It's possible to have a rent review combination of CPI plus a fixed increase; for example, 'CPI + 1 per cent'. It's best to avoid CPI-only increases, as this can potentially minimise your rental growth (especially if CPI turns negative).

Fixed increases

Fixed increases in rent give certainty to the landlord and the tenant, but as mentioned, can sometimes mean the rent becomes out of alignment with the fair market rent over a long-term lease. Typically, fixed increases are either 2 per cent, 3 per cent or 5 per cent a year.

Market review

Most leases will have an allowance for market rent reviews during the term of the lease or upon the exercise of options. After the market review at the start of a lease or the exercise of each option, the lease will have either fixed, CPI increases or a combination of both.

The landlord generally determines the market rent at the stage of the market review, but the tenant can dispute the figure. If they do this, a valuer may be brought in to supply a rental valuation report. This will compare the average rent per square metre with other rental properties in a similar location to calculate what the rent should be. In most leases, the valuer's determination is final and binding on the two parties. Typically, the new rent level cannot be less than the rent payable for the years before the review: this should be stipulated in the lease. During economic crises, it's also common for landlords to assist tenants by allowing for lower rent, to protect the long-term prosperity of both parties.

Turnover rent

Turnover rent is generally the method used in large retail shopping centres for evaluating rent. The figure will be a percentage of the turnover of the business operated from the leased premises. This is often used in addition to a partial fixed-rent amount.

The tenant is responsible for providing audited financial statements monthly to show their turnover. Strict provisions govern how landlords can use this turnover information, including how and to whom the information can be provided. The reason that shopping centres typically use this method is that it allows them to have a useful mix of tenants, as smaller businesses are able to afford the rent. This mix will ultimately lead to increased variety of customers and increase foot traffic to their complex.

Weighted average lease expiry

Weighted average lease expiry (WALE) is a commonly used measurement to determine the average years of lease left on a multi-tenanted commercial property or your entire portfolio. Some other abbreviations that are used are WALT (weighted average lease term), or WAULT (weighted average unexpired lease term). These are most common in the US and Britain. WALE gives a numeric figure of how a multi-tenancy property is performing as a whole unit, as opposed to individual tenancies.

The WALE is measured by either the tenant's income or the tenant's lettable area against the total income or total area of the other tenants. If the property had only a single tenant, the WALE would simply be the number of years left on the lease. It's important to analyse both WALE types, depending on the type of property being purchased. For example, a shopping centre could have a large area WALE if it has an anchor tenant on a 10-year lease. Typically, though, an anchor tenant pays a lower rental rate that could result in a lower rental WALE.

Lenders will look favourably on a high WALE, because it generally means a lower risk investment spread across multiple tenants and guarantors.

Commercial properties with a higher WALE (four or more years) will generally have larger blue-chip tenants – usually businesses that are established and can commit to a longer tenancy. Lower WALE properties will have shorter leases and usually a higher turnover of tenants, because they're usually small to medium-sized businesses and cannot commit to three or more years. Smaller businesses typically go one of two ways: either they outgrow the space and move on, or they aren't profitable and don't continue with their lease.

A lower WALE will mean higher leasing costs in agent fees, periods of vacancy, advertising fees, incentive payouts, legal fees and valuations. This could have a significant effect on the long-term performance of the property. However, a shorter WALE can be beneficial if you are looking to upgrade the property or renegotiate lease agreements.

How to calculate WALE

To see how WALE is calculated, let's look at an example: a small retail strip of four shops in a suburban area of Brisbane, Australia.

EXAMPLE: Calculating WALE for a small shopping strip

Property details

Total lettable area:	450 m²
Annual gross rent received:	$135,000
Area WALE:	3.17
Rental WALE:	3.25

Tenancy, income and lease details

Tenant details	Lettable area	Annual rent	Remaining lease term
Property 1 Supermarket	200 m² 44.4%	$62,000 (45.9%)	5.0 years (60 months)
Property 2 Barber shop	50 m² 11.1%	$19,000 (14.1%)	2.5 years (30 months)
Property 3 Bakery	100 m² 22.2%	$27,000 (20.0%)	2.0 years (24 months)
Property 4 Takeaway shop	100 m² 22.2%	$27,000 (20.0%)	1.0 years (12 months)
Total	450 m² (100%)	$135,000 (100%)	

Area WALE calculation

The area WALE in the example is calculated by multiplying each tenant's area percentage by the remaining lease on their tenancy and then adding these figures for all the tenants together. So, tenant 1, the supermarket, has 44.4 per cent of the lettable area and 5.0 years remaining on its lease – multiplying the two figures – 44.4 per cent by 5 – equals 2.220. For all four tenants, the equation is as follows:

$(44.4\% \times 5) + (11.1\% \times 2.5) + (22.2\% \times 2) + (22.2\% \times 1)$
$= 2.220 + 0.278 + 0.444 + 0.222$
$=$ Area WALE of 3.17 years

Rent WALE calculation

The rental WALE is similarly calculated, by multiplying each tenant's percentage of rent by their remaining lease term. For the example, this is as follows:

$(45.9\% \times 5) + (14.1\% \times 2.5) + (20.0\% \times 2) + (20.0\% \times 1)$
$= 2.295 + 0.353 + 0.400 + 0.200$
$=$ Rental WALE of 3.25 years

With area and rent WALE both at more than three years, this appears to be a strong investment for its size and location – but let's look at the net yield and other factors as well.

Yield, cash flow and property advantages

We can calculate the net yield, as discussed in Chapter 6, by dividing the property's net income by its value:

Yield calculation

Purchase price: $1,875,000
Net rent: $135,000
Net yield: $135,000 ÷ $1,875,000 = 7.2%

Now, let's look at the property's cash flow:

Loan amount: 70% at 5% interest rate
Interest repayments: $1,875,000 × 70% × 5% = $65,625
Cash flow: $135,000 − $65,625 = $69,375

This property, without depreciation, has a cash flow of close to $70,000 a year! (More details about cash-flow calculations can be found in Chapter 11.) The property also has a number of advantages:

- a corner location
- multiple tenants
- it's freestanding and has future development potential
- high-density housing is being constructed across the street
- low competition in the area
- high foot traffic
- a growing population in the region.

This example shows how a passive income can be generated quickly through one very low-risk, versatile asset. Income will only increase over time with rental increases, and with that comes capital growth.

Sample lease schedule

To close this chapter, here's an example of lease particulars and a lease schedule, so you can get an idea of what these might look like if and when you make your own commercial property purchase.

Sample lease schedule

Item 1.	**Base rent**
	$70,000.00 per annum plus GST

Item 2.	**Base rent review dates and type of review**	
	Review date	**Review type**
	On each anniversary of the commencement date	3%

Item 3.	**Tenant's proportion (of outgoings paid)**
	$11,540.00 excluding GST.

Item 4.	**Permitted use**
	Commercial kitchen (with ancillary café)

Item 5.	**Option(s) for renewal**
	2 × 5 years

Item 6.	**Guarantor(s)**

Item 7.	**Amount of bond or bank guarantee**
	4 months' base rent plus GST, which on the commencement date of the lease is $25,667.00.

Item 8.	**Amount of public risk insurance**
	$20 million

Item 9.	**Rent review dates and types of review at the start of and during the option(s)**	
	Review date	**Review type**
	For the first year of the option(s)	Market review 3%
	For the second and subsequent years of the option(s)	

Item 10.	**Lawyers for landlord**

Item 11.	**Lawyers for tenant**

Item 12.	**Address of premises**

Sample lease table of contents

CHAPTER EIGHT
OUTGOINGS

Outgoings are expenses that a landlord incurs directly from owning a property. As mentioned in Chapter 7, depending on the terms of the lease, the owner or tenant can be responsible for paying them. These costs can make a big difference to a tenant's or owner's bottom line and must be accounted for; in this chapter, we'll look at the most typical outgoings on a commercial property.

Council rates

Council rates are a type of property tax to cover the cost of public or community services such as the running of the council; construction and maintenance of roads, bridges, kerbing, parks and gardens and council buildings such as libraries; community activities and advertising; tree and bush management; and pest eradication.

Local councils use property values to calculate how much each owner pays in rates – in other words, how much you pay will depend on the land value of your property. The council will estimate the 'unimproved value' of your land to calculate your rates. (Unimproved land value is the dollar figure a block of land is deemed to be worth by the council without any buildings or structures on it. It's calculated based on its location and comparable vacant land sales.) If you think the valuation is not in line with other properties in the area, you can lodge a complaint, as this could directly affect your land tax bill should you be over the threshold.

Council rates are paid quarterly in advance. Some councils offer discounts for early payment, so it's worth checking this. Exemptions from rates can apply to Crown land, land used for religious purposes, charitable land, and land used for mining or forestry.

Land tax

Land tax is a state-based tax that applies to investment properties in your portfolio, excluding your principle place of residence (PPOR). It applies when the total taxable value of the unimproved land you own is above the threshold for the Australian state or territory they are located in; this land-tax threshold is reviewed yearly in each state. There are different thresholds for personal and company ownership structures.

Land tax doesn't just apply to commercial properties, of course: it applies to other investment properties such as residential property and vacant land as well. Land tax applies regardless of whether income is earned from the land.

Property-management fees

Property-management fees are charged by a real estate property manager for managing the property. We'll talk about these in detail in Chapter 28.

Water and utility rates

Water rates are paid to the authority that provides water and sewerage services to your property. The rates are paid quarterly in arrears and have two components: a fixed amount for providing the water mains to the property, and a variable amount based on your water usage. There's usually no discount for early payment.

Utility rates include electricity and gas and they are usually separately metered. If the building has common areas that require electricity for lighting, for example, the strata manager will have a separate contract with an electricity provider. These fees are usually passed on to the tenant. There can be quite a cost variation among utility companies, so shop around. Most will offer a discount if you sign a longer agreement, too.

The tenant is usually responsible for the water and utility rates.

Body corporate fees

A body corporate may be called an 'owners corporation' or 'strata corporation', depending on where you live, and is the entity that manages the common property of a building or complex. Body corporate fees cover everything from building insurance and maintaining common areas through to shared utilities, building works and repairs.

The funds the owners contribute each year form the body corporate or strata committee budget. They are generally divided between an administrative fund which mainly covers day-to-day expenses and a sinking fund which pays for emergencies, capital works and irregular, large-scale works. Sometimes a special levy is required if unexpected costs arise that weren't considered when the administrative and sinking fund budgets were set.

Body corporate fees are calculated by adding the total amount required to maintain and manage the building for each year, and dividing that among the owners depending on their proportion of ownership. The fees are agreed on at the annual general meeting (AGM), in which all owners in the building can vote.

Insurance fees

Insurance protects the owner's asset should something unexpected happen. The three main insurances required on a commercial property are:

1. building insurance

2. landlord insurance

3. public liability insurance.

Building insurance covers the physical building against damage. The property should be insured for as many items as are applicable to your area, including, for example, fire, flood, storm, earthquake, hail, bushfire and third-party damage. If the property is freestanding (i.e. not attached to another building), it's imperative to have building insurance. Most lenders will require you to have it, in fact, before they'll give you finance.

If the property is strata titled, the body corporate will hold the building insurance for the common areas of the property. However, it's best to check what the body corporate insurance covers. The tenant isn't always responsible for the building insurance, so it's important to check what's stipulated in the lease. In strata buildings, the tenant or occupier is responsible for insuring the contents.

Landlord insurance will cover the owner's loss of rent should the property become uninhabitable after damage caused by a natural disaster. Rent cover isn't usually the responsibility of the tenant, so it's up to you, as the owner, whether to take this out. The decision will usually come down to your financial position and risk profile, and the risk on the property itself.

Public liability insurance protects the owner from being sued if someone is injured on the property. Most tenants will have this, but check. It's rare that the owner pays for public liability insurance unless they are responsible for common areas.

Maintenance costs

All property types require general maintenance. Tenants are usually responsible for maintenance inside their premises, but the complex will be looked after by the owner or the body corporate. Maintenance costs are often left out of real estate agents' presentations because they are usually for one-off items such as repainting the building.

The tenants will normally be required to maintain and repair the property, but not to make large capital expenditures such as replacing an air-conditioning unit. It's important to stipulate the tenant's responsibility for maintenance in the lease, as then, if they fail to fulfil their maintenance duties, the costs for replacement can be passed onto them.

Gardens and landscaping

Gardening and landscaping may be a fairly low-cost feature or, in a bigger commercial complex, more extensive or elaborate and a lot more expensive to maintain. Before buying a property, it's worth obtaining the gardener's details to find out how much work is required and whether there are any extra costs coming up, such as tree removals or garden upgrades.

Cleaning

Cleaning of the tenant's premises and the shopfront is, of course, the tenant's responsibility. For the common areas, including the walkways, washrooms, rubbish bins, lawn, yards and car-park areas, many multi-tenanted commercial properties have a third-party cleaner. Typically, when an investor buys a property, a cleaner will already be servicing the premises.

Find out the details of the cleaner's contract, such as the frequency of cleans, the length of time and the cost. If you feel there are cheaper options, it's worth bringing this up at the next body corporate meeting. Getting the best value-for-money deal you can for cleaning can reduce outgoings for the tenant or owner.

Fire inspections

It's essential that your commercial property complies with the latest fire regulations. Most governing bodies and councils will require an inspection annually, biannually or quarterly, depending on your commercial property type, and penalties can apply if these aren't performed in accordance with the code.

Fire inspections are conducted by a third-party company, and will include inspection of evacuation plans, exit signs, smoke detectors, extinguishers, fire hoses, fire hydrants, fire doors and the building cladding compliance. An annual fire compliance certificate is provided that needs to be kept and recorded; if the property has a strata manager, it will usually organise this.

Since the Grenfell Tower fire in London in 2017, fire safety has become a big focus. The fire was caused by a faulty fridge, but really was an issue due to the combustible cladding. Buildings with this cladding are now pretty much uninsurable for public liability coverage and can have orders for expensive removal and refit with safer material. This has prompted bans on many materials, so it's essential to check this point before buying.

Backflow prevention testing

Backflow prevention devices are fitted to water pipes to prevent the reverse flow of potentially polluted water from a property back into the mains supply. Some devices require testing by a licensed company. The local council will outline how often your backflow devices need to be tested – usually yearly. As with fire inspections, there are penalties for non-compliance.

Rubbish removal

For most commercial premises (excluding mixed-zoned residential properties), rubbish removal is not provided by the council. It's usually organised by the tenant or by the building's strata manager if there is one. Rubbish removal can cause arguments among tenants, as different businesses produce differing amounts of waste. As an owner, you'll need to monitor how much rubbish is removed and how often, to ensure you're not paying for a service that's not required.

CHAPTER NINE

DEPRECIATION

Depreciation is the loss in a property's value over time as a result of ageing and wear and tear. You can obtain substantial tax and depreciation benefits from commercial properties. Although owners of residential properties can also claim depreciation, it's more significant for commercial buildings because they're generally larger and typically have a more expensive construction and fit-out. A concrete office building, for example, will depreciate more than a timber residential home due to the increased cost of materials and construction.

Commercial property owners can claim deductions for the fall in value of the building's structure, as well as the fall in value of any assets they own within it. Commercial tenants can claim deductions for the decline in value of any assets they bought or installed during the fit-out.

It's worth noting that the land itself cannot be written off and its cost is not deductible.

Calculating depreciation deductions

Depreciation deductions can be broken down into deductions for the buildings structure (known as capital works) and for plant and equipment. Let's go into these in more detail now.

Capital works

'Capital works' refers to the building's structure and any items considered permanently fixed to the property, including the building itself and any structural improvements. Capital works can be written off over a longer period than other depreciating assets.

In Australia, the capital works deduction is available for:

- buildings or extensions, alterations or improvements to buildings

- alterations and improvements to leased buildings, including shop fit-outs and leasehold improvements

- structural improvements such as sealed driveways, fences and retaining walls

- earthworks for environmental protection, such as embankments.

If it's not possible to determine the actual construction costs, you can get an estimate from a quantity surveyor or other independent qualified person. You can claim a deduction for the full estimate from the year the cost was incurred.

Deduction rates of 2.5 per cent or 4 per cent apply, depending on the date on which construction began, the type of capital works, and how they're used. It's worth noting, however, that even investors who buy commercial properties built before the threshold dates are often able to claim capital works deductions on renovations to the property.

Plant and equipment

'Plant and equipment' are assets that the Australian Taxation Office (ATO) deems easily removable, or those that are mechanical. These include air conditioners, refrigeration, ovens, fans, carpets and so on. The depreciation of assets within a building is calculated on an individual basis in accordance with each asset's value and its longevity – which is determined by the ATO each year and referred to as an asset's 'effective life'.

Commercial property investors can claim depreciation on any assets they own within the property, but not on anything the tenant installed as part of their fit-out.

If the asset is worth less than $300, you can claim an immediate deduction in the income year that you bought it. If not, you use one of two methods to calculate an asset's annual depreciation:

1. **The diminishing value method** gives you higher claims in the first few years and smaller claims later on, as the value of most items reduces this way.

2. **The prime cost method** gives you equal tax deductions each year over the course of an asset's effective life. The prime cost method is also referred to as 'straight line' depreciation.

When purchasing a property, it's advisable to have a quantity surveyor produce a tax depreciation schedule (TDS) as soon after settlement as possible. This will ensure the surveyor assesses the property in the exact condition you inherited it and will deliver the most accurate depreciation estimates. Then, it's essential to review and update your depreciation schedule if you do significant renovations. Each item in your property will have a specific depreciation percentage which will be outlined in this schedule.

When you're considering whether to buy a property, ask the selling agent for the previous owner's depreciation schedule. This will give you an accurate indication of the added cash flow from depreciation. It's worth noting here, though, that you should never buy a property based solely on the tax benefits – the fundamentals of the purchase need to be sound!

CHAPTER TEN

CAPITALISATION RATE AND PROPERTY VALUE

Capitalisation rate or 'cap rate' is a concept used to determine a property's market value at that moment in time. In simple terms, a cap rate is often calculated as the ratio between the net operating income (NOI) produced by an asset and its original capital cost (purchase price only). So, if you purchased a property for $1 million and it returns $50,000 in net rent per year, it has a cap rate of 5 per cent.

Cap rates are different from cash-on-cash returns (annual return versus cash invested into the property): they're based solely on a property's net operating income and purchase price, without adjusting for any debt, mortgage repayments or purchasing costs such as stamp duty. This means you can do a direct comparison with other properties. Cash-on-cash returns and return on investment (ROI) are explored further in Chapter 11.

Capitalisation rate and net yield are essentially the same thing, and often used interchangeably. The main difference is that the term 'net yield' is often used for the net return of the property, whereas investors commonly use the term 'cap rate' to compare the value of commercial properties using their rental yields. Cap rates are useful for doing a quick back-of-the-envelope calculation to compare the relative value of similar commercial properties, however a detailed cash-flow analysis should be performed when considering buying an individual property.

The cap rate can be used in a number of ways to help you compare investments and remove the guesswork from buying and valuing properties. In addition, much like net yields (as you saw in Chapter 6), the cap rate can be reversed to calculate a purchase price for a property. With rental increases and a stationary cap rate, you can work out an approximate new value for your property. For example, let's say you buy a property for $1 million with a cap rate of 7 per cent and annual rental increases of 3 per cent:

Property purchase price: $1,000,000
Capitalisation rate: 7%
Rental increases: 3%

If the cap rate in a region remains unchanged, you can see that the value of the property will increase considerably with rental increases alone:

Year	Rent	Property value
1	$70,000	$1,000,000
2	$72,100	$1,030,000
3	$74,263	$1,060,900
4	$76,491	$1,092,727
5	$78,786	$1,125,509
6	$81,149	$1,159,274
7	$83,584	$1,194,052
8	$86,091	$1,229,874
9	$88,674	$1,266,770
10	$91,334	$1,304,773

In 10 years, the property is worth more than $300,000 more, just from steady 3 per cent rental increases.

The cap rate varies for different commercial asset classes as well as the region they are located in.

Cap rates are also influenced by the lending environment and the cost of borrowing – lower or higher interest rates will affect cash flow and hence can influence the property's cap rate over time.

You can find out what the cap rates are by:

- **Asking the property agent.** A selling agent or property manager will be able to give you a quick gauge of cap rates, as they will know their area well. To get accurate information, though, it's best to speak with agents who aren't involved in the sale.

- **Checking sold prices.** You can obtain comparable cap rates by checking the recent sales history of similar properties and finding out what the properties are renting for.

- **Checking local property advertisements.** Some agents will advertise the property based on a net yield, which will give you an indication of some competing cap rates.

- **Speaking with a local valuer.** A local valuer is a great independent source without an ulterior motive. Their job is to check cap rates to obtain an accurate valuation.

Match your property's type and location with the best information you can get from the four sources in the list. It's unlikely an advertisement will tell you what the property will sell for, so it's up to you to find recent sales to use for negotiation.

Reasons for lower cap rates

Cap rates are lower in properties that have strong tenants, national franchises, high foot traffic, solid locations such as beachfronts, capital cities, or areas with low vacancy rates, as these are seen as lower risk or higher capital-growth areas. If the property is free-standing, the land value may reduce the cap rate.

Reasons for higher cap rates

Properties with a higher cap rate may be in a quiet area or a regional town, have low foot traffic, high vacancies, a short lease or a short time left on the lease, a poor-quality tenant, a startup tenant or one in a dying industry. These are perceived as higher risk or likely to have low capital growth. Higher cap rates may appear attractive from the outset, but once you take into account the longer periods of vacancy, leasing fees, marketing costs, incentives, and lower capital growth their net result is usually less.

Valuation methods

Commercial property investors use three main methods to value properties:

1. income
2. comparable sales
3. replacement cost.

Income method

The income method is the most commonly used method by investors whose primary objective is cash flow. Once the data – mainly income and outgoings – is obtained and verified, the property's net income can be calculated. The cap rate is then calculated and compared with the market cap rate. This gives a good indication of the value of the property, assuming the tenant is paying fair market rent.

Comparable sales method

This method uses previous comparable recent sales to estimate a property's value, and is usually done for the previous six months.

It can be taken over a longer period, however, if there have been no big changes in cap rates in the area, or if there have been few sales – say, if the area is quite regional.

You can pay a valuer to assist with this and to do a short-form valuation. The valuer will inspect the property and compare it to recent sales in the area.

Business owners who are looking for vacant commercial space will typically use this method, because they're less interested in the cap rate and rents. They want only to ensure they're buying a well-priced, comparable vacant property – this is often done by comparing the square-metre rates of similarly sized commercial investments.

Replacement cost method

The replacement cost method is mainly used as a backup verification and for newer properties. You first determine the land value and then the cost to replace the building. This is much easier to quantify with newer properties, as depreciation needs to be considered for an older building. Note that this method doesn't take into account the strength of the lease and the cap rate.

The formula for the replacement cost method is as follows:

Estimated value = land value + the building cost
– depreciation

Vacant properties

Valuing vacant properties can be more difficult than valuing tenanted ones. You'll first need to research what level of rent the property will bring, by comparing similarly sized tenanted properties and calculating the rate per square metre. You then apply this rate to the floor space of the vacant property to obtain a rental estimate. You also need to assess how long it will take to find a tenant, by speaking with local real estate agents and property managers. It's best to be conservative in this, because rent and vacancy periods can change depending on the time of year or external influences. Finally, you may need to assess how much renovations will cost to get the property up to scratch for leasing or any rental incentives that will be required for new tenants.

CHAPTER ELEVEN

CASH FLOW

Cash flow is one of the largest considerations for an investor buying a commercial property. The cash flow is the income the property produces after all expenses. So:

Cash flow = net income – mortgage repayments
– all expenses to the owner

There are pre-tax and post-tax cash flows, as depreciation and tax benefits may affect the result. Let's look at how cash flow is calculated in detail, using the example of a regional dental clinic that was bought as an investment.

EXAMPLE: Calculating cash flow for a regional dental clinic

Property details

Purchase price:	$900,000
Deposit:	30%
Deposit total:	$270,000
Loan amount:	$630,000
Stamp duty:	$30,600
Additional purchasing costs:	$3,000
Total acquisition costs:	$303,600
Loan interest rate (interest-only loan):	5.00%
Net yield:	7.00%
Net rent:	$63,000

Note that the example assumes the property is being purchased tenanted; if it were purchased vacant, there would be additional costs such as renovations, lending costs, and paying the rates until a tenant moves in and begins paying.

Return on investment

Return on investment (ROI) is a measure used to evaluate the efficiency of an investment or to compare the efficiency of a number of investments. ROI directly measures the return on a particular investment compared to its cost. It's sometimes referred to as 'cash-on-cash return' – this usually refers to the return based purely on cash flow, however, whereas ROI also considers the investment's capital growth.

Using the dental clinic example again, let's compare the ROI when we have rental increases, which should equate to capital growth with an unchanged cap rate.

EXAMPLE: Calculating ROI for the dental clinic

		Year 1	Year 2	Year 3	Year 4	Year 5
Expenses	Loan interest	$31,500	$31,500	$31,500	$31,500	$31,500
	Outgoings	$0	$0	$0	$0	$0
	Miscellaneous	$0	$0	$0	$0	$0
	Yearly expenses	$31,500	$31,500	$31,500	$31,500	$31,500
Cash flow	Rent 3% increases	$63,000	$64,890	$66,837	$68,842	$70,907
	Depreciation (prime cost)	$5,000	$5,000	$5,000	$5,000	$5,000
	Total cash income per year (pre-tax)	$31,500	$33,390	$35,337	$37,342	$39,407
	Total cash income per year (post-tax)	$36,500	$38,390	$40,337	$42,342	$44,407
Equity	Increased property value at 3% growth	$900,000	$927,000	$954,810	$983,454	$1,012,958
	Equity	$0	$27,000	$54,810	$83,454	$112,958
ROI Accumulated cash flow	ROI (acquisition costs) pre-tax	10.38%	21.37%	33.01%	45.31%	58.29%
	ROI (acquisition costs) post-tax	12.02%	24.67%	37.95%	51.90%	66.53%
ROI Accumulated cash flow and capital growth	ROI (acquisition costs) pre-tax	10.38%	30.27%	51.07%	72.80%	95.50%
	ROI (acquisition costs) post-tax	12.02%	33.56%	56.01%	79.39%	103.73%

To calculate ROI, the benefit (or return) of an investment is divided by the cost of the investment, and the result is expressed as a percentage or a ratio. In our dental clinic example, you can see that the ROI for the first year of the investment was 10.38 per cent pre-tax – so, the total pre-tax cash income that year ($31,500) divided by the acquisition costs ($303,600). As you can see from property value in the 'Equity' row of the table on page 97, there was no capital growth in that year, so it's not included in the calculation.

You can see that over five years, with 3 per cent rental increases and 3 per cent capital growth, the accumulation of the cash flow and the available equity mean the dental clinic's ROI becomes quite high. Having a 95.5 per cent ROI pre-tax in five years is a great outcome and this will only be enhanced with lowering interest and cap rates.

The table opposite shows what the ROI will be with interest rate fluctuations and different loan to value ratios (LVRs). The LVR will be different if you use a larger deposit, pay cash or leverage your purchase against another property. It's possible to have a 100 per cent LVR – that is, to borrow 100 per cent of the property's price – if another property's equity is being drawn on to finance the purchase.

You can see that at lower interest rates, borrowing more enables you to maximise the ROI on the cash flow. However, being highly leveraged has risks. If there are high interest rates, the ROI can become negative, and if the property became vacant, there would be more of a financial stress on the owner in regards to cash flow. With a high LVR such as 100 per cent (using another property's equity for the deposit), if there were a market drop in prices, this would put the owner into a negative equity position – which would mean if they sold, they would require funds to pay off the mortgage. It's important to factor in your personal circumstances and risk appetite when deciding on which LVR to obtain. This is discussed in depth in Chapter 13.

Pre-tax cash flow ROI	Loan interest	Capital required	Cash flow (rent less interest)	ROI from cash flow
Cash purchase	$0	$933,600	$63,000	6.75%
50% LVR @ 5% interest	$22,500	$483,600	$40,500	8.37%
70% LVR @ 5% interest	$31,500	$303,600	$31,500	10.38%
100% LVR @ 5% interest	$45,000	$33,600	$18,000	53.57%
50% LVR @ 7.5% interest	$33,750	$483,600	$29,250	6.05%
70% LVR @ 7.5% interest	$47,250	$303,600	$15,750	5.19%
100% LVR @ 7.5% interest	$67,500	$33,600	-$4,500	-13.39%

Paying down a commercial property loan

With the regional dental clinic example, what happens if you decide to pay down the principal loan by putting the cash flow back into the property's debt?

As you can see from the table overleaf, when paying down a property, the yearly cash flow will increase as the interest repayments reduce each year.

In the eleventh year the property will become debt free and the following year have an unencumbered (free of debt) $92,000+ of yearly cash flow. In addition to this, the investor would have achieved significant capital growth. This shows the power of commercial property investing when compared with residential property.

Year	Loan interest if paying off	New yearly cash flow (post-tax)	Amount of debt remaining
1	$31,500	$36,500	$593,500
2	$29,675	$40,215	$553,285
3	$27,664	$44,172	$509,113
4	$25,456	$48,386	$460,726
5	$23,036	$52,871	$407,856
6	$20,393	$57,641	$350,214
7	$17,511	$62,715	$287,500
8	$14,375	$68,107	$219,392
9	$10,970	$73,837	$145,556
10	$7,278	$79,923	$65,633
11	$3,282	$86,385	$-
12	$-	$92,207	$-

CHAPTER TWELVE
CAPITAL GROWTH

Much like the residential property market, the commercial market moves in cycles. The commercial market's cycles generally lag behind the residential cycles, however, mainly due to the much longer locked-in leases. Commercial tenants are likely to tough out the hard times because the penalties of walking out on their lease are higher than those for residential tenancies, and because their livelihood depends on the property.

Within the overall market cycle, of course, the capital growth of different commercial properties can vary a lot depending on demand for the property and its type, purpose and location. In any case, it's wise to have a long-term mindset when you're buying commercial property due to the high entry and exit costs. If you do your due diligence correctly, you can mitigate most market fluctuation risks and so profit in the long term. (We'll explore due diligence in detail in Part V.)

Note that large national companies moving into a suburb or area is a good indicator for future growth. These businesses spend a large amount of money researching areas so as not to risk losing their capital investment in the property should the business not prosper. On the other hand, cheap airline flights into the region can indicate that demand for and migration to the area are falling.

Let's examine the different phases of capital growth in the market cycle in a bit more detail.

The market cycle

Here's a diagram illustrating the cycle of the commercial property market clock, with slow down, recession, recovery and boom phases:

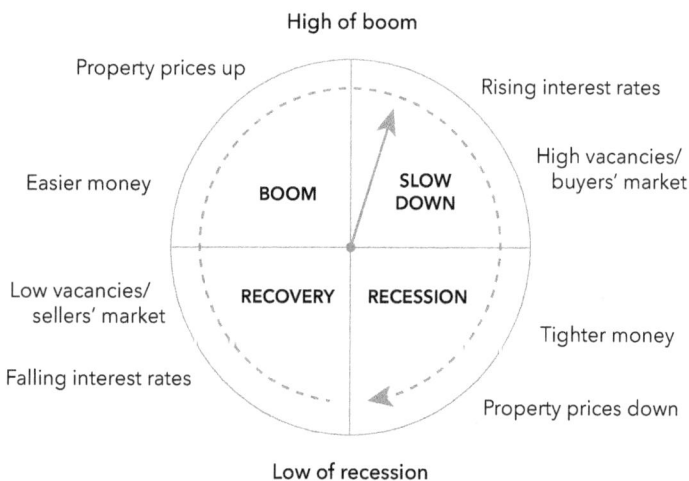

Slowdown

The slowdown phase is characterised by an increase in new construction and slow increases in vacancy rates as developer's new constructions come on to the market, leading to oversupply. The rise in vacancies can also be due to a pullback in demand caused by a shift in the economy.

Rents continue to rise, but more slowly. This becomes a buyer's market, as there's more stock available than is being bought. As more properties are listed online and more 'For lease' and 'For sale' signs go up in an area, rents will begin to fall. Some investors will decide to sell during this phase because of the risk of a recession.

Recession

In a recession, vacancy rates rise substantially as yet more new properties hit the market. Landlords offer rent concessions to try to retain tenants, causing rents to become more competitive. Developers who are late to the game will start offloading stock at below-market prices before the recession really hits. As the supply becomes saturated, prices will stagnate for a while and rent growth will be negative or below the rate of inflation.

This is a great time for investors to buy at highly discounted rates, with the aim of holding the property longer term and waiting for the next boom.

Recovery

The recovery phase is characterised by high vacancies and no new construction. Occupancy levels are near or at their low, and rental rate growth is either negative or flat, as owners offer rent concessions to avoid the occupancy rate falling further. As the population grows or market conditions improve, more businesses move into the area, vacancy rates will tighten and the market will begin to grow again.

It's possible to pick up a bargain-priced property during the recovery phase and hold it for two to four years until the boom phase. It's best to buy a fundamentally solid property in a great location and to capitalise when rents increase and leases are renewed, and it may be wise to look at refinancing the property in the next phase to extract equity if you're looking to grow the portfolio.

Boom

A boom or expansion phase is characterised by falling vacancies. Demand pushes up rent and yields, leading developers to start building commercial properties; the most capital growth occurs in this phase. This is typically a seller's market, but buyers may be able to profit from the climbing market by purchasing properties with current deficiencies at a discount and repositioning them to sell on or refinance. Some common examples include finding rundown properties and renovating, finding properties for which tenants are paying below market rent and increasing the rent, moving tenants on short leases to longer leases, or even changing the tenant completely to a more attractive business.

Growth in gross domestic product (GDP) is usually back at normal levels. At the high point of the boom, supply and demand are evenly matched. When developers release their new stock, there'll be more movement among tenants as they seek more competitive rents.

The cycle of market emotions

Emotion plays a huge role in the real estate industry and can be responsible for huge swings of market growth or decline (see figure opposite). When optimism, excitement, fear, panic and hope are involved, booms and recessions can occur with no real economic stimulation. Humans generally act in a herd mentality, which can snowball these effects. Similar to the market cycle, these emotions can be location or asset-type based.

During a rise in property prices, optimism and excitement build. As the cycle approaches its peak, emotions are at the highest point, as most people in the market are making money and there are a lot of buyers. This is a seller's market; the buyers will generally lose out in the coming years.

As prices begin to fall, many buyers who have ridden the wave start to feel anxious; as the market continues to drop, fear increases and some owners will look to sell to minimise their losses.

This becomes a buyer's market, with more buyers than sellers. When the property price approaches the bottom of the cycle, there is even more fear, and the doom and gloom will be reflected in media reports.

Many buyers and sellers rely on the way the share market functions to guide them when buying or selling a commercial property. This approach normally instils fear in the buyer, rather than confidence, and can be a trigger for some of the cycle of market emotions. A 5- to 20-year approach should be taken, no matter what market you are in, and you should assess the current and long-terms risks.

Eventually, however, the market will begin to rise and optimism and excitement will re-emerge.

The cycle of market emotions

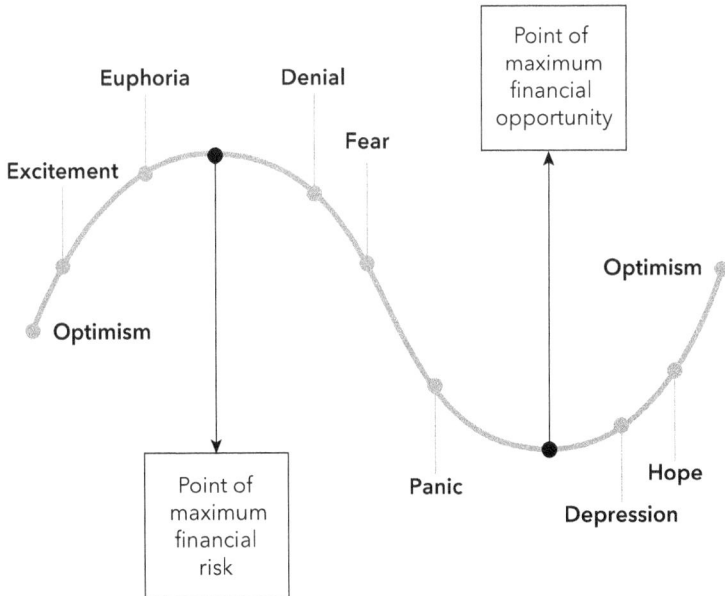

Growth factors

Let's take a look now at the factors that affect capital growth for commercial property, feeding both the market cycle and the cycle of emotions. In residential property, capital growth is somewhat one-dimensional: driven by supply and demand. Commercial properties are influenced by many other factors as well, with some of the broader key indicators being the overall economy, interest rates and government spending on infrastructure. At the individual property level, the property's attributes, the tenant, the length of the lease and changes to the rent or the cap rate can all affect capital growth. Let's explore these in a bit more detail.

The economy

A strong or strengthening economy is fundamental for a rise in commercial property prices. As the economy starts to grow, demand will increase. First, there'll be more demand for warehousing due to the need for storage, supply and fabrication. This will be followed by rising demand for retail space, as consumers feel more confident and begin to spend more; the flow-on from this confidence will be increased demand for office space. An economic downturn, by contrast, can present the opportunities of lower priced properties, which will allow optimum returns.

Some of the economic factors that affect property values are:

- gross domestic profit (GDP)
- wage growth
- unemployment rates
- household savings rates
- migration rates
- changes in taxes or tax rates
- changes in the overall population.

Interest-rate changes

Lending interest rates can directly affect a commercial property's price, as they will change the cash flow from the property. A lower interest rate will increase the cash flow; hence, buyers will be willing to pay more for the same property. Cheaper credit then flows into capital expenditure and commercial property investment. At the time of writing, commercial real estate provides a higher yield than residential when compared to borrowing rates.

Conversely, when the Reserve Bank raises interest rates to manage inflation and slow the economy, the higher cost of money slows the rate of growth. At the same time, higher rates tend to reduce consumer spending, which can slow demand for both commercial and residential property.

Infrastructure spending

The development of infrastructure and new freeways can change the demand for commercial property. Increased access to a region means cheap land and good roads, with resulting urban sprawl and an increasing population. This spurs yet more infrastructure spending and provides an impetus for transport companies to move their warehousing facilities to the area.

An area with an increasing population requires more services, and as the new region develops, businesses will move in and different types of commercial properties will be built to service demand.

Individual property factors

The specific attributes of a property can also, of course, determine its value. Key points such as the age of the building, its services and location can all influence demand, and if the property has development potential or the council zoning changes, this can instantly affect its value. Properties that are zoned from low-density to a higher density instantly increase in value, as they gain developer appeal.

Tenant and lease length

The tenant and the lease length also influences the property's value. As a tenant approaches the end of the lease period, confidence in the property can drop – and hence the price will fall too. On the other hand, if the tenant has just exercised an option or signed a long lease, this can improve confidence and increase the property's price.

The type of tenant can also play a part in buyer confidence and the likeability of the property. Obtaining a new multinational, blue-chip tenant can make the property hugely more attractive as an investment proposition and lower the cap rate.

Rental increases and cap rate

With rent changes, if the cap rate of the area remains the same, rent increases will directly and proportionally change the property's value. Conversely, if the cap rate changes due to the growth factors mentioned earlier, this too can affect the property value. Let's return to our dental clinic example and run the numbers for it.

You can see that rental increases and variations in the cap rate directly affect the property value. The aim is to always buy in a region or a style of property with an increasing demand and a lowering cap rate, as this increases the value dramatically.

Now, let's move on and look at how you can grow your investment portfolio in order to achieve your overall goals.

EXAMPLE: Calculating the impact of rent increases and cap rate

Property details

Purchase price: $900,000
Net yield: 7.00%
Net rent: $63,000

Cash flow

	Year 1	Year 2	Year 3	Year 4	Year 5
Rent 3% increases	$63,000	$64,890	$66,837	$68,842	$70,907
New property value @ cap rate 7.0% (initial)	$900,000	$927,000	$954,810	$983,454	$1,012,958
New property value @ cap rate 5.0%	$1,260,000	$1,297,800	$1,336,734	$1,376,836	$1,418,141
New property value @ cap rate 9.0%	$700,000	$721,000	$742,630	$764,909	$787,856

CHAPTER THIRTEEN

GROWING THE PORTFOLIO

As you saw in the previous chapters, quite a few factors affect a commercial property return. Capital growth and the return from the cash flow are fundamental when you're expanding your property portfolio.

Expanding your portfolio quickly comes down to the basics of compounding leveraging. Compound returns occur when you earn a return on an investment and then reinvest those proceeds, thereby increasing your earning power. In other words, if you earn a percentage income on the capital you've invested, that income is then added to the amount you began with. The new total amount then earns more income in the next period, and this accelerates the growth over time, as you're earning 'income on the income'.

For example, if you invest $100,000 at a 7 per cent per annum interest rate and it's compounded monthly, in 10 years you'll end up with $200,966 – as you can see in the diagram on the next page.

Real estate is one of the few investments which lenders will let you leverage significantly, and when you combine compound returns with leveraging, you can achieve growth on a much larger scale. As you saw in Chapter 11, you can generate a very high cash-on-cash return.

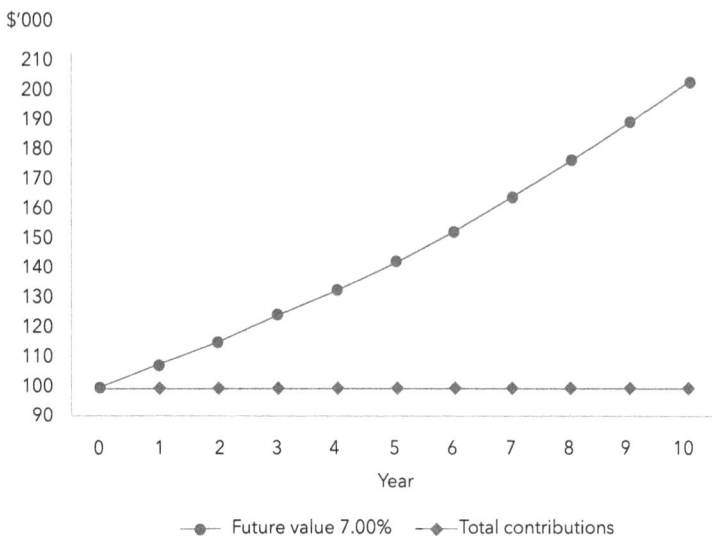

$'000

—●— Future value 7.00%   —◆—Total contributions

It's worth noting again that you need to beware of the potential negative effects of leveraging, though. Be cautious about taking on large amounts of debt – while the positive returns can be great, you'll also magnify any losses. Maintaining a comfortable loan to value rate (LVR) is crucial for portfolio risk mitigation. For the most part, lenders are likely to keep you in check, but this isn't always the case with private lenders or vendor finance.

Considering leverage

When deciding how much to leverage, you'll need to consider a number of factors:

- **Your risk appetite.** How much money can you risk – how many dependants and commitments do you have? Ask yourself how much cash or equity you need and how aggressive you'll be with your investing. If you're a high-income earner with a large amount of liquid savings, for example, you can take on more risk than a low-income earner with minimal savings.

- **Your goals.** Developing a strategy will come down to your individual short-, medium- and long-term goals. I spoke about goals in the 'Why commercial property?' introductory chapter: remember, your goals should be based on what truly makes you happy. Don't chase a particular passive income number or asset number for the sake of it: be realistic about what you want and what you're prepared to sacrifice to achieve it.

- **Your time frame and exit strategy.** It's important to consider your time horizon – the period in which you'd like to expand the portfolio to achieve your desired cash flow. Also, think about your exit strategy. Will you need to sell one or more properties to obtain cash or to pay off a principal place of residence at some point?

Remember, a property's performance and/or the market conditions may not live up to your expectations, so purchase with a margin of safety. Not every property in your portfolio will be an outstanding performer – there are too many market variables to get everything right in the long term, although focusing on getting as many fundamentals right as possible will minimise this risk. It's also essential to stress-test your portfolio. This involves checking how your portfolio would perform at higher interest rates or with periods of vacancy, and ensuring that you can financially handle these situations.

Another point to take into consideration is that one of the most common mistakes investors make is not having sufficient cash reserves for unexpected expenses. If or when a property becomes vacant, you need a buffer to be able to pay the rates, mortgage and any other expenses. Choose a buffer amount that's appropriate for you – your risk profile, how many properties you own, your responsibilities, your income and the typical vacancy rate of the properties in your portfolio. We'll look in more detail at how to cope with downturns in Chapter 30.

A 10-year example plan

Let's look at a sample portfolio now so you can see how it could be expanded. This is a 10-year plan, based purely on commercial properties and steady rental growth. Note: this is just an example! In real life, personal circumstances and factors outside your control will speed up or slow the process, including cap rate changes, interest rate changes, valuations, capital growth, lease renewals, vacancies and ease of lending.

Let's say you were to buy a commercial property costing $900,000, using a 30 per cent deposit, and that you have an extra $30,000 per year that you can put into your portfolio. The details are as follows:

Interest rate: 5% (with interest-only repayments)
Rental increases: 3%
Cap rate: 7%
Additional yearly contribution: $30,000

Take a look at the table on pages 114-115. You can see that within three years you'd be able to buy a second property worth $650,000, using the cash flow from the first property, the capital growth from the rental increases, and your $30,000 of annual savings. You do this by using the savings plus refinancing the first property back up to an LVR of 70 per cent. You'd then have two properties growing in value and a higher cash flow that could enable you to buy a third property in year seven, and a fourth in year nine.

You can see from the table that after 10 years, you could theoretically end up with a portfolio worth $4.5 million plus – returning a passive income of $160,000 without depreciation. The portfolio will continue to grow with the market, so the passive income will remain relative to the costs of goods and services.

Note that the portfolio can expand rapidly over time, so the more properties you accumulate in the early stages, the larger your portfolio can be. The biggest regret for most investors is not buying sooner. However, there's a saying: 'While the best time to plant an apple tree was 10 years ago, the second best time is today'. Of course, picking the market is important, but a long-term approach is needed. Most countries have a diverse property market with markets operating independently of one another in each major city. The fundamentals still apply: don't buy the same asset as everyone else is buying. Don't follow the herd. Look at properties on their merits.

It's best to focus on long-term benefits, not short-term gains. This includes looking at the net position each year and not cutting corners to save on minor yearly costs.

You may be able to accelerate your portfolio expansion by:

- buying well – that is, securing a property at well below market price

- adding value – whether by simply renovating the property or by undertaking more elaborate measures (Chapter 29 has more information on this.)

- increasing rents – this can have a huge effect on the portfolio, as it increases cash flow and capital growth.

Year	Property	Property value	LVR	Loan amount	Rent	Cash flow	Accumulated cash flow	Additional contributions	Growth equity	SUM cash flow + contributions + 70% equity
1	Property 1	$900,000	70%	$630,000	$63,000	$31,500	$31,500	$30,000	$0	
2	Property 1	$927,000	68%	$630,000	$64,890	$33,390	$64,890	$60,000	$27,000	
3	Property 1	$954,810	66%	$630,000	$66,837	$35,337	$100,227	$90,000	$54,810	$228,594 used for deposit of Property 2
4	Property 1 (refinance 1)	$983,454	70%	$688,418	$68,842	$34,421	$34,421	$30,000	$0	
	Property 2	$650,000	70%	$455,000	$45,500	$22,750	$22,750	$0	$0	
5	Property 1 (refinance 1)	$1,012,958	68%	$688,418	$70,907	$36,486	$70,907	$60,000	$29,504	
	Property 2	$669,500	68%	$455,000	$46,865	$24,115	$46,865	$0	$19,500	
6	Property 1 (refinance 1)	$1,043,347	66%	$688,418	$73,034	$38,613	$109,520	$90,000	$59,892	$341,541 used for deposit of Property 3
	Property 2	$689,585	66%	$455,000	$48,271	$25,521	$72,386	$0	$39,585	
7	Property 1 (refinance 2)	$1,074,647	70%	$752,253	$75,225	$37,613	$37,613	$30,000	$0	
	Property 2 (refinance 1)	$710,273	70%	$497,191	$49,719	$24,860	$24,860	$0	$0	
	Property 3	$975,000	70%	$682,500	$58,250	$34,125	$34,125	$0	$0	

Year	Property	Property value	LVR	Loan amount	Rent	Cash flow	Accumulated cash flow	Additional contributions	Growth equity	SUM cash flow + contributions + 70% equity
8	Property 1 (refinance 2)	$1,106,886	68%	$752,253	$77,482	$39,869	$77,482	$60,000	$32,239	
	Property 2 (refinance 1)	$731,581	68%	$497,191	$51,211	$26,351	$51,211	$0	$21,308	
	Property 3	$1,004,250	68%	$682,500	$70,298	$36,173	$70,298	$0	$29,250	
9	Property 1 (refinance 2)	$1,140,093	66%	$752,253	$79,807	$42,194	$119,676	$90,000	$65,446	$545,798 used for deposit of Property 4
	Property 2 (refinance 1)	$753,528	66%	$497,191	$52,747	$27,887	$79,098	$0	$43,256	
	Property 3	$1,034,378	66%	$682,500	$72,406	$38,281	$108,579	$0	$59,378	
10	Property 1 (refinance 3)	$1,174,296	70%	$822,007	$82,201	$41,100	$41,100	$30,000	$0	
	Property 2 (refinance 2)	$776,134	70%	$543,294	$54,329	$27,165	$27,165	$0	$0	
	Property 3 (refinance 1)	$1,065,409	70%	$745,786	$74,579	$37,289	$37,289	$0	$0	
	Property 4	$1,555,000	70%	$1,088,500	$108,850	$54,425	$54,425	$0	$0	

Portfolio size: **$4,570,839**   Yearly cash flow: **$159,979**

PART IV
BUYING AND SELLING PROPERTIES

Part III covered the numbers you need to run in order to be able to assess a property investment and make a plan for expanding your portfolio and achieving your goals. Now, let's look broadly at the steps involved in buying and selling properties:

- preparation
- searching for properties
- the acquisition process, and
- selling and exit strategies.

After this overview of the process, we'll go into the nitty-gritty of the due diligence you need to do before you purchase, in Part V.

CHAPTER FOURTEEN

PREPARATION

So, you've decided commercial property is right for you. You understand the different types and the numbers used to analyse commercial property investments, and you want to get started. Here are six useful steps to take to prepare:

1. Assess your current financial position.

2. Work out your purchase price range.

3. Decide whether you're a passive or active investor.

4. Set some goals.

5. Develop a plan.

6. Build your team.

1. Assess your current financial position

First, you need to know your current financial position:

- **Cash on hand.** How much cash do you have to invest?

- **Income.** What is your income? How stable is your employment? What is the longevity of your paid employment?

- **Cash flow.** Analyse your present cash flow from your assets – property, cash, shares, businesses, superannuation and so on – compare this to your liabilities. Do you have property or business loans? Car loans? Credit cards or personal loans? What are your financial family commitments?

- **Borrowing capacity.** Speak with a broker or lender to find out how much you can borrow.

- **Credit rating.** Find out your credit rating. In Australia, there are three reporting agencies from which you can obtain your credit rating report: Equifax, Illion and Experian.

- **Your risk profile.** Analyse your risk profile, how much buffer would be required and how much financial stress you can handle. A financial adviser can help with this.

2. Work out your purchase price range

The second step is to work out what sort of price you'll be able to pay for a property, based on your current financial position. Speaking with a broker or lender can give you an indication based on your personal circumstances. Assuming you have borrowing capacity, if you're using cash savings a quick check is to work backwards and divide that figure by 0.35 to work out a possible purchase price. The 0.35 represents a 30 per cent deposit plus about 5 per cent in purchase costs.

If you have a surplus of cash, it may be possible to look at properties that require immediate renovations so you can achieve a quick equity gain and reinvest.

If money is tight, a lower-priced tenanted property that is cash-flow positive from the start may be best versus waiting for a higher-priced one. Buying two cheaper properties over time would have the benefit of diversifying your asset types and their locations as well as having two tenants. Weigh up whether it's better to buy a cheaper property or two now or wait until you can afford a more expensive one that may be of higher quality. This will depend on how quickly you can save more money, as sometimes getting into the market sooner will have a better net result than waiting and saving, since you could be missing out on capital growth which may be more than your rate of saving.

3. Decide whether you're a passive or active investor

Next, think about whether you'd be best as a passive or an active investor:

- A passive investor wants the property to perform as well as possible with a minimal investment of time.

- An active investor has the time and the inclination to be closely involved in searching for a property and adding value to it.

You need to know where your time is best spent – for example, working for an income or in a business startup – and how much time you have available in a day. If you've decided you're an active investor but don't have enough time to devote to the process, engaging a buyer's agent could be a good option. My clients engage me to do the legwork for them: researching properties, running the numbers and then presenting them with different purchase options. We'll discuss buyer's agents further in step 6, 'Build your team'.

4. Set some goals

As I've mentioned before, your goals will depend on where you are in your life, your risk profile, how aggressive you want to be, what you want to achieve (portfolio size, cash flow and so on), and over what time frame. Also, remember that your goals cannot be only about the money – what will make you happy while you're building wealth and after you achieved the level of wealth you'd like?

You need to envisage the long term and plan for it, but there are so many life variables that the long term is hard to predict. So, you need realistic short- and medium-term goals – focusing on these will give you the best chance of achieving your long-term goals. Write down your goals, be flexible along the way, and reward yourself as you reach each milestone. A buyer's agent or financial adviser will be able to assist you with setting these goals.

5. Develop a plan

We looked at an example 10-year plan for growing a property portfolio in Chapter 13. Developing your own plan is about looking at the numbers required to reach your goals, then working backwards from there. It can be helpful to consult a financial adviser, at this point, to draw on their experience and knowledge and ensure your plan is achievable. Exit strategies are an important part of this plan and are further explored in Chapter 17.

6. Build your team

Purchasing commercial property isn't something you can or should do solo: choose a team of trusted individuals to assist you through the process. There are multiple ways to find your team; referrals and online searches are the most common. However, one of the better methods is to find successful investors and ask them who they use. It will be less likely that a very successful investor has a weak team. When vetting individuals and teams, look at their qualifications, of course, but also consider:

- Do you like them? This is very important, as is the reverse – because if they like you, they're more likely to work harder for you.

- Do they sound competent and confident?

- Do you feel you can trust them? Assess what personal benefit they'll get from your business.

- Do they have good communication skills, and do you feel they'll deliver when they say they will?

If you can, try to speak with the person's previous clients, who'll usually be happy to share their views. It is important to understand how they differentiate themselves from their competitors. You can ask the adviser to provide the details of some previous clients to discuss this.

A great finance broker or bank manager, accountant, buyer's agent, solicitor, property manager, town planner and valuer can be worth their fees many times over. A mentor of some kind (paid or unpaid) can also be invaluable.

Let's look now at what each of these advisers do and why you may need them.

Finance broker or bank manager

You need a finance broker or bank manager who has extensive experience in commercial lending. Many residential brokers will say they also do commercial transactions, but you need someone experienced to ensure you get the best rate and lender for your situation, as there are commercial-only lenders who may be able to finance you when the major lenders will not. More details on financing are provided in Chapter 24.

Be wary of finance brokers who try to upsell you circuitously related products such as life insurance and/or who aren't focused on getting the best mortgage deal for you. A good broker will be able to tell you the shortcomings of different deals – such as the break costs of a lower interest rate deal – and why and when to avoid these, depending on your strategy. They should focus on your agenda, not theirs.

Accountant

An accountant with experience in dealing with large-portfolio clients is essential. She or he will be able to tell you which structure is best for buying each property, depending on its purpose and cash flow. Please note, though, that accountants aren't financial advisers, so investment advice outside the realm of tax should be questioned, as they may have ulterior motives.

Mentor

It's always great to have someone to discuss each commercial property deal with – whether that's someone highly experienced, an online forum, or a buyer's agent. Just make sure that the person you choose as a mentor has bought many properties outside of where they live, so they have a truly in-depth knowledge of commercial property. A paid adviser such as a buyer's agent can also act as a mentor.

Buyer's agent

Buyer's agents are the opposite of the selling agent: they represent the buyer. They can handle the whole research and purchasing process for you, which is very advantageous if you're inexperienced, nervous or time-poor. A buyer's agent's service includes:

- sales and data research
- due diligence
- recommending building and pest inspectors, conveyancers and property managers
- negotiation of property purchases, and
- supporting you through the purchasing process.

A buyer's agent will also often have access to off-market properties. As a buyer's agent myself, of course I think we are well worth our fee. You'll learn from our expertise, see more quality properties, save time, and be able to negotiate a better price with selling agents.

Buyer's agents work on a commission basis, but be aware that they have minimal liability if they buy you a poor-quality property – so it's critical that you find an ethical agent who has many positive reviews.

Solicitor

Most solicitors are generalists or experts in one certain area of law: it's crucial that you have a highly competent property solicitor who is experienced in commercial property acquisition, leasing and due diligence. There are even solicitors who specialise in each of these fields.

It's also imperative that the solicitor has a hands-on approach and doesn't pass your purchase on to be handled by a paralegal or conveyancer. Don't just choose the cheapest solicitor you find – buying a commercial property is a major investment and it's important to have the right person on your team. So, before you engage someone, ask them how many commercial deals they've done and if they can provide any references.

Note that if you're buying in different states in your country, it's usually best to use a solicitor from the state the property is in – it's even better if they're in the same region or town, because they'll have more local knowledge.

More details about conveyancing are provided in Chapter 23.

Property manager

Local property managers are another great source of information: they'll be able to quickly give you the cap rates and typical vacancy periods of similar properties to those you're looking at. More about this in Chapter 28.

Town planner

Town planners are responsible for the design and development of towns and cities, and understand the ins and outs of council regulations and policies. Having access to a knowledgeable town planner in the area you've selected to purchase your property is therefore invaluable for value-add projects like developments, subdivision or renovations. Without an experienced planner, specific conditions could be overlooked and this could magnify the costs of a development project if your application is rejected. It's best to choose an independent town planner rather than one provided by the local council. Independent town planners are generally more up to date, spritely, and willing to give information, as they'll hope that you will utilise their services at some stage.

Valuer

Property valuers estimate the value of your property by looking at comparable sales, estimating the land value, and looking at development potential and the demand for the type of property. It's their job to estimate the price you could realistically achieve for a property if it was given reasonable marketing. With this knowledge, experienced commercial property valuers are a great source of information – they know their area well and will offer unbiased information.

***

Once you've completed these six steps and have a skilled team of advisers on board, it's time to jump in and start looking for investment properties!

CHAPTER FIFTEEN
SEARCHING FOR PROPERTIES

After doing your research and determining the general locations and types of properties you're interested in, you can start looking at properties in your price range. You can also look at properties at, say, $100,000 more than your price range, as you may be able to negotiate that down, or the price may drop if the property doesn't sell.

It's unlikely you'll find a property that you consider 100 per cent perfect; the aim is simply to find one that meets your satisfaction criteria as closely as possible.

How to find a property

There are three basic ways to find properties:

1. via real estate websites

2. through real estate agents

3. through buyer's agents.

If you establish good relationships with real estate agents in regions you favour, they'll contact you about potential properties. (A buyer's agent, if you engage one, will have existing relationships with selling agents.)

When you're using websites such as realcommercial.com.au, you can speed up your search by using filters for location, budget and types of commercial property. The map view on these websites is a good way to choose a location – and also shows you how many similar properties are available in the area for sale.

It's also worth checking Google's satellite images to look for potential greenfield developments in the area, and comparing the Google Street View with the property advertisement photos.

Due diligence on each property can take a lot of time, so it's critical that you make a short list. Narrowing your wish-list to a few areas, and to the specific types of commercial property you're interested in, will help prevent you getting an overload of properties. You can then choose a few to visit and make an offer on.

Note, in some states of Australia it's possible to go under contract without viewing a property in person, because it will be subject to inspection and due diligence clauses.

After you enquire about a particular property, the selling agent will send you an information memorandum (IM).

Information memorandums

An information memorandum is a sales document used to advertise the property and give critical information about it. It will include photos, description of the property, tenant information, investment highlights and location highlights. It will also contain a disclaimer waiving responsibility on the part of the agent if any of the figures are incorrect, so it's imperative that you crosscheck all figures as part of the due diligence process. Remember, the selling agent will show only the positives and will hide the negatives.

There is a phrase in contract law, 'Caveat emptor' – Latin for 'Let the buyer beware'. It applies to most real estate purchases and when a sale is subject to it, the purchaser assumes the risk that the presented information may be incorrect.

Pro formas

A pro forma is a projection of a property's financials, but not its actual financials. Sellers or selling agents may present pro formas in the information memorandums to demonstrate potential future value, but it's unwise to take these into account in your calculations, as they're not guaranteed. Instead, you should create your own pro forma when analysing a property, and not share this with the seller. Your pro forma may include physical or operational changes, such as future renovation works to increase value, new tenants or higher rents. Work out the return on investment (ROI) from the changes you may make to see if they'd be viable and how they would benefit you.

Methods of sale

The method of sale will dictate the way in which you will put offers on properties, the terms of the contract, and the order in which due diligence and finance will occur prior to going under contract. The selling agent will inform the potential buyers of which method of sale is likely to be used.

Expressions of interest

Expressions of interest (EOI) aren't binding, but you need to be aware that they can sometimes stipulate conditions that need to be adhered to should the actual contract be signed. This could include, for example, paying the seller's solicitor's fees.

On an EOI, you specify your buying entity, your offer, the amount of deposit and terms you would like in the contract such as due diligence and settlement. Your conditions may entice a buyer, for instance, if you're paying cash. You don't have to have completed your due diligence when you submit an expression of interest, but you still need to allow time for it. Bear in mind that due diligence can take a lot longer if it's a multi-tenancy property.

Some EOIs have closing dates and are used to gauge interest before an auction. Agents will often put pressure on you to come up with an offer, and might also play other buyers off against one another. EOIs can turn into a silent auction: interested parties are required to put their best offer in writing by a certain time and date, and the property is then sold to the highest bidder. A Dutch auction evolves when a property is listed for private sale and multiple buyers agree either to pay the advertised purchase price or a price that the vendor will accept. With a Dutch auction, the vendor has to agree to sell at the level of one of the offers and therefore has nothing to lose in seeking a higher price. It's advisable to stay away from Dutch auctions, as they're rarely advantageous to the buyer in terms of achieving a good purchase price.

The benefit of an EOI, however, is that you can negotiate seriously without having to spend money on legal fees and valuations.

Fixed price listings

The fixed price sales process is the most common method. Such listings may be indicated on websites by wording such as:

- 'Price on application'

- 'Offers above $1,200,000'

- 'Contact agent'

- 'High yielding, 7 per cent net yield, $1,200,000'.

It's wise to check whether properties advertised this way have previously failed to sell at auction or been advertised for a long time.

Generally, a fixed price listing produces a quick sale without the seller having to pay expensive auction costs or lose time on an expression of interest process. It also enables the seller to have the contract ready subject to finance, which allows for many potential buyers. However, it can be a slow process if there are many buyers or the owner isn't desperate to sell. The ideal situation is a desperate seller who is more likely to accept a lower-than-market price offer.

Fixed price listing encourages open communication with the owner through the sales agent – you can work indirectly with them so that the sale benefits both parties. It means you can put forward your concerns to the seller to help with negotiating.

Off-market sales

Some owners are happy to sell privately, for a number of reasons; for example, they may not want tenants, friends, family or neighbours knowing the property is for sale. A private sale also reduces advertising costs and may mean a quicker sale if the selling agent has good contacts.

A good way to find off-market properties is to develop good relationships with sales agents, perhaps after you've made an unsuccessful offer on another property. Buyer's agents will also know of large numbers of off-market properties.

The process for negotiating an off-market sale will usually be the same as for a fixed price listing, with communication via the sales agent.

Note that just because the property is off-market doesn't mean it's better value. Your due diligence process will remain the same.

Auctions

Auctions are generally held for very attractive properties, such as those in the CBD or those that have national brands as tenants; they're less common on cheaper properties. This is a high-risk method of buying and should be left to knowledgeable investors.

You should complete the same level of due diligence (as outlined in Part V) before you make an offer at auction as when you're using the other methods, including getting unconditional finance approval and paying for valuations. If you don't or can't go through with the purchase after winning an auction, you inevitably will lose your deposit and potentially remain liable for any further losses and damages sustained by the seller – auctions are legally binding.

A 10 per cent deposit is due immediately after a successful auction. A smaller deposit can be negotiated before the auction, but this will usually incur legal costs that aren't recouped if you lose the auction. Lenders will usually give you the funds for a deposit at an auction if you're using other properties as security, but this can come at a higher interest rate during the settlement period.

***

Once you have compiled your short list of properties, you need to do your due diligence on these – as mentioned, we look at this process in Part V. After your due diligence is complete, it's time to start negotiations on the properties that still appear to be a good investment for you.

CHAPTER SIXTEEN

THE ACQUISITION PROCESS

The acquisition process involves three main stages:

1. negotiations
2. the 'under contract' period
3. settlement.

1. Negotiations

Negotiations on a property can take a day or months, depending on the seller and how much back and forth there is. Both the price, and the terms and conditions can be negotiated as part of the process. These negotiations are usually performed through the selling agent (unless it's a private sale directly with the owner) and can be formal or informal, verbal or written in the first instance.

It's worth pointing out that making an offer on a property is not a legal commitment (except at an auction) – it's only an indication to the agent that you're interested.

The art of commercial property investing comes down to confidence. If you use the right negotiating style, selling agents will want to work with you because they believe they can secure a deal.

Let me reiterate here that before you start negotiations, it's important that you know the area well, are aware of comparable sales and rents, have spoken with the tenant, know how long the property has been on the market and have carried out your initial due diligence (covered in Part V). All this information can all be used to reduce the price. Know what the cap rates and yields are before you negotiate, as well.

Even though the agent represents the seller, she or he will, as I mentioned, want to work with you to secure the sale. The agent will highlight how good the tenant is, the growth potential of the property, other buyers' interest and that there are higher offers. You, by contrast, should focus on the negatives, using some of the details the tenant has given you, or that you've uncovered from the research you've done.

Check how long the property has been on market, and whether it has failed at auction. If it has failed at auction, there may be some opportunity to make a lower offer. Try to find out why the owner is selling. Is it a rushed sale? Can you work with them to reduce the price? Note that although distressed sales do come up, they're rare and often you'd be better off finding a solid deal elsewhere. You need to know the level of demand for the property you're interested in, too, as high demand will limit your negotiation power while low demand and high supply will increase it.

You're more likely to obtain a quick purchase, of course, if it's a cash purchase and the sale is not subject to your obtaining finance. For this, it's important to know the demand for the type of property.

Your greatest strength in negotiation, however, is to be able to walk away from the deal. The agent will want to work with you and will chase you, and being overly keen can be detrimental to your position. Sometimes, the agent may even tell you the lowest price the seller will accept, which will reveal how keen the sellers are to sell and whether they have unrealistic expectations. Some agents will indicate very high prices to the seller to get them to sign with their agency and then, if the property is on the market for a month or two, bring down the seller's expectations at that point. It's quite reasonable for you to point out that the owner's expectations are too high.

The negotiation usually ends somewhere between the seller's expectation and the buyer's initial offer, so it's helpful to understand the seller's needs. They may not agree to a lower price, but may consent to terms and conditions that suit you, such as a longer settlement. These are the usual negotiable terms when making an offer on a property:

- price
- rental guarantees
- early access (usually for building maintenance or showing prospective tenants through)
- finance periods
- vendor finance
- building and pest inspection access
- due diligence periods
- deposit amount
- subject to development applications.

A few notes about these:

- After you have exchanged contracts, the deposit is usually 5 to 10 per cent of the purchase price. You will get it back if you pull out of the contract over conditions such as due diligence or finance. If you exit the contract not under a condition and it's during the cooling-off period (usually the first five days), you'll lose 0.25 per cent of the purchase price. If you pull out after the cooling-off period, you can be liable for your full deposit as well as any damages caused to the seller.
- With regards to rental guarantees, it is possible to negotiate these on commercial properties – usually when you're buying

new from a developer and they want to reassure you of a cash flow. As you'd expect, they're more common during a buyer's market. A rental guarantee can assist you with obtaining finance from a lender, as well, but take care when reviewing the lease to ensure your interests are protected.

- In Australian tax law, a vacant commercial property is not deemed a 'going concern' and 10 per cent GST will be applicable on the purchase price. Once tenanted, you should be able to claim the GST on your BAS (business activity statement); however, it's advisable to speak with an accounting professional before buying.

- You can negotiate a longer lease as part of settlement with the tenant. This is known as an 'agreement to lease', and will become effective at the time of settlement. An agreement to lease can help with obtaining finance, because lenders look favourably on longer leases.

- You should document all communication. Even if you have phone discussions with real estate agents, it's essential to have a soft copy of all communication as a backup and for record keeping. This applies even after you have bought a property.

- If any information is found to be incorrectly presented, this should be a reason for you to go back and negotiate the price, if applicable.

- It's also possible to make a deal subject to a development application and approval. If a property has been on the market for some time, the seller may be open to this. The development could be for adding tenancies, for instance, or converting the premises from industrial to retail. You do need to be sure that your application would be approved, as if it isn't, you can lose money on council application fees. If it goes well, though, it can be very beneficial, as you might get a higher rent than the one on which the seller based the sale price. Alternatively, having an approved development application can simply increase the value of the property.

Both seller and buyer need to feel they have negotiated a good deal, so try to reach a win-win solution, and follow up your verbal offer on a property with an email to the agent. Never become emotionally involved or committed to making the purchase, and don't get defensive if it doesn't go your way. Looking at multiple properties at the same time, rather than focusing on one property, will make this easier. Mentioning other properties that you're looking at can encourage the selling agent to try to secure a deal, too.

If you walk away from a purchase, tell the agent why and what price it would need to be to attract you, as the property may stay on the market and the agent may come back to you later. Also, ask the agent to keep an eye out for similar properties – this actually encourages them to work with you on the first deal as well as subsequent deals.

Showing common courtesy to the selling agents if your offer isn't accepted is crucial. Being polite doesn't show weakness – rather, it shows that you're confident, understand the process and aren't emotionally invested. This may encourage the selling agent to want to work with you in the future and even send you properties prior to them hitting the market.

2. The 'under contract' period

Before you sign the contract, your solicitor will do a quick review of it; they will examine it more closely once it's signed (assuming there are exit conditions). Then, you need to:

- arrange conveyancing – covered in Chapter 23
- organise a building and pest inspection – see Chapter 21 for more on this

- organise finance – which we'll go into in Part VI
- perform due diligence – explored in Part V.

Try and minimise the legal, finance and due diligence costs by first doing the items that are free, such as area and tenant research. Building and pest reports, valuations and searches cost money. Never stay in a deal just because you've invested some funds, though – the due diligence costs are minimal compared with the financial hit you'll take by purchasing an unsuitable property.

3. Settlement

Before you settle on a property, it's essential that 1) you're satisfied with it and 2) you're prepared for settlement day. Your solicitor will ensure most of the legal and registration matters are taken care of, but you need to arrange the following:

- **Organising insurance.** If something happens to the property between exchange of contracts and settlement, having adequate insurance will give you peace of mind. In most states in Australia, the risk of the property passes to the buyer one day after the contract date.

- **Collecting keys, passes and codes.** Make sure you know who has the keys and when you can collect them from the agent or your lawyer. Also, make sure you have the alarm codes (if any) and instruction manuals. Some buyers want to collect the keys from the agent on the day of settlement; others have the keys delivered to their solicitor after settlement. By sorting out the logistics beforehand you can ensure there are no delays or problems later.

- **Arranging a pre-settlement inspection.** This is to ensure the property is in the same condition as when you performed your earlier inspections. For vacant commercial properties, this is critical to ensure no damage has occurred or rubbish been left behind. Even if the property is tenanted and the tenant is responsible for the property, an inspection is still recommended, though it's not essential. Normally, your property manager will arrange it free of charge, as they will use the meeting to introduce you to the tenant.

- **Organising cheque directions.** Your solicitor will organise the settlement cheques on your behalf, but it's up to you to make sure the amounts and payees are correct before settlement day. If funds that are to be borrowed are coming from a lender, the lender must have the authorisation present to draw on these funds. The solicitor will also calculate the adjustments required for rates and other council fees. Note that the seller is responsible for these up to and including the day of settlement, and these costs are usually calculated pro rata to the date of settlement. Make sure that the cheques have the correct spellings to avoid delays.

If you have finance on the purchase, on settlement your lender will draw down on your loan. This means the lender will debit the amount paid on your behalf from your loan account. Once settlement is completed, you or your property manager can collect the keys from the agent and take possession of the property. We'll look at the process of managing the property in Chapter 28; but now, let's look at the process of selling a property.

CHAPTER SEVENTEEN

SELLING PROPERTIES

Selling a property is a tough decision. Ideally, you want to hold on to your properties long term, as they're delivering you an income. So, before you consider selling, run the numbers carefully and calculate your return on the property, taking into account the stamp duty, purchasing costs, selling costs and capital gains tax. Remember, if you're planning to sell the property and replace it with another, you'll need to pay stamp duty and purchasing costs again – and this can add up to more than 10 per cent, just to change one property for another.

You might choose to sell:

- when it's a seller's market – that is, there are lots of buyers in the market and you can achieve a top price

- if the market looks to be heading into a downturn, it may be worth selling before the herd is aware (remember the market phases we looked at in Chapter 12?)

- when interest rates are rising, because cap rates will fall

- if you believe that rents won't increase in the near to medium future and there are better opportunities available to you

- when selling is part of an exit strategy – we'll look at this in more detail later in the chapter.

Obviously, you might also choose to sell if you get a great offer for the property – say, for example, if a developer offers an above-market price.

Here are some reasons not to sell:

- if it's a buyer's market
- if the area the property is in is gentrifying and has growth prospects
- if interest rates are dropping
- if the market is still growing.

Don't sell a property just because you don't 'like' it, either – commercial investing is about the numbers! Let's say, however, that the value of the premises has grown significantly and you need funds to invest in a better project. Ask yourself:

- How does selling fit into my plan?
- Where will I put the profits?
- How leveraged is my portfolio?
- What's my risk profile?
- What's my exit strategy?

Preparation for selling

If you do decide that selling is a wise idea, there are a few preparatory steps that will help you achieve the best price:

- Increase the rents to market value if you haven't already done so, if a fresh lease or option has just been signed.
- Try to get tenants on leases that are as long as possible.

- Make cosmetic improvements to the property. Fresh paint, for example, upgraded flooring or a revamp of the landscaping (if there are garden or lawn areas) might help present the property in its best light.

- Reduce operating expenses by, for example, looking for cheaper insurances or regular maintenance services.

Exit strategies

When you're investing in property of any kind, you need to have an exit strategy before you begin. We touched on exit strategies in Chapters 13 and 14: choosing one should be part of your preparatory planning. Each investor's exit strategy will be different, depending on their goals, their portfolio and personal circumstances; a financial planner may be helpful here, in providing advice on what could be most appropriate for you. Your strategy may change as your circumstances alter, but it can guide the decisions you make along the journey.

The following are the seven most common exit strategies you could use when looking to capitalise on your investments:

1. Keeping all your properties and not paying down the debt.

2. Keeping all your properties but paying down the debt.

3. Keeping all your properties and increasing your debt.

4. Selling part of your portfolio to pay down debt.

5. Selling part of your portfolio and living off the profit.

6. Selling your whole portfolio.

7. Selling some properties by vendor finance.

Let's look at each of these in turn.

1. Keeping all properties and not paying down debt

Keeping all your properties and not paying down your debt is the fastest way to build a passive income, but it also carries quite a lot of risk. Generating a passive income from accumulation is the key focus, rather than paying down the debt. Once you have an adequate portfolio and your desired cash flow, you stop buying more properties, and even though you maintain the same level of debt, over time the properties will probably increase in value. As rents increase, but the mortgage amount stays the same, your passive income will increase. The risk with this strategy is you can be exposed to property price swings, and will also be more financially affected if the properties become vacant.

Some people may decide to pay down the debt slowly, using any surplus cash flow but in this strategy, it's not the main focus: the principal objective is to generate a passive income to provide financial freedom.

2. Keeping all properties but paying down debt

If you keep all your properties but pay down the debt, you stop buying properties before retirement so that you leave enough time for the cash flow from the properties and your own savings from your employment to accumulate enough to pay off the debt. You can achieve the same cash flow as in the first strategy with a smaller portfolio size, because once the loan is paid off you don't have the interest expense to pay. Once you own the portfolio outright, too, most of the risk is mitigated as there's no debt. This will make it easier to manage even a vacant property.

3. Keeping all properties and increasing debt

The third strategy involves continually refinancing your properties in order to live on the extracted equity. Instead of living off a purely passive income (generated only from cash flow), you're also living off capital growth – as your properties go up in value over time, you can draw portions of that increased equity to live on. However, to maintain the same passive income, you'll need your rents to go up enough to counteract the increased repayments required due to the equity withdrawal. With this strategy, you need a larger portfolio to generate enough cash flow to keep servicing your loans.

This is the highest risk strategy as it's the most susceptible to market cycles, vacancy levels and lending fluctuations.

4. Selling part of your portfolio to pay down debt

Selling part of your portfolio and using the proceeds to pay down the debt on your remaining properties when you retire from formal employment is the most common strategy. Obviously, you need to have multiple properties; usually, the plan is to sell lower-yielding properties to pay off the higher-yielding ones and maximise the cash flow for your retirement.

Most investors will stagger the selling of the properties over several years, in order to minimise capital gains tax liabilities.

5. Selling part of your portfolio and living off the profit

This strategy involves selling your properties in stages and living on the proceeds; it's typically used by investors who need a higher income. The downside of this strategy is that every time you sell a property, you reduce your passive income and miss out on any future capital growth.

6. Selling the whole portfolio

Selling your whole portfolio is usually part of a conservative strategy in which the funds are placed in a low-risk savings account to provide an income during retirement. Some people may diversify their profits into other investments to mitigate risk. This is quite a rare strategy, as property is generally seen as a stable investment, depending on the type and location. Sometimes, an investor may instead use the profits to buy into lower-risk real estate – moving from commercial to residential property, for example, to lessen the chance of long-term vacancies.

Investors will sometimes choose this strategy if they have enough superannuation to live on and want to give the proceeds from property sales to family members.

7. Selling some properties by vendor finance

Selling properties via vendor finance is a strategy for investors who would like to sell some properties but still retain a portion of the passive income from them over a fixed period. The buyer will pay back the owner in a similar fashion to a lender, however this is typically performed over a shorter period of time. Vendor finance is explained in detail in Chapter 25. It can also be used to minimise capital gains tax upon selling, or when you don't want to sell an entire property. Any of the first six strategies can be used in combination with vendor finance, but receipt of the proceeds will be staged.

***

Think carefully about your exit strategy, and perhaps consult a financial adviser if you feel it would be helpful, to make sure you consider all the relevant issues.

Now that you have a good overview of buying and selling, we're going to take a deep dive into the details of due diligence, in Part V.

PART V
DUE DILIGENCE

As I've mentioned before, due diligence is the most important part of buying a commercial property. It's a lot of work, but is essential to determine whether a property is a quality asset. The purpose of due diligence is to discover current or potential problems with a property, understand its upside, and verify the information obtained. This will help you negotiate the correct price for the property.

Due diligence for a commercial property is much more detailed than for a residential one. A poorly selected commercial property can become a real liability, whereas you can buy a poorly priced residential property and, as long as it's fundamentally suitable and in a good area, it will still make a positive return on investment long term.

In this part of the book, we'll look at area research, tenant and business analysis, and building and pest inspections, then Chapter 22 wraps it up with a handy detailed checklist you can use.

CHAPTER EIGHTEEN

INITIAL DUE DILIGENCE

Some investors perform only cursory due diligence, and accept the data provided in the Information Memorandum as gospel. It's crucial not to assume anything, though: all facts and figures need to be crosschecked. Undertaking thorough due diligence can reduce the stress of a purchase, give you more confidence, and ensure your negotiation skills are first class. Your analysis needs to be at least as good as, if not better than, the lender's valuation.

Having said that, it's easy to get analysis paralysis with due diligence, so take a high-level view first. Many investors become too focused on insignificant issues that stop them making a quality purchase, and complicate and lengthen the buying decision. No property is perfect: just run as many numbers as possible to determine whether it's a sound investment. The fundamentals of due diligence are the same whether you're buying a $300,000 or a $30 million commercial property.

When you're starting out, as mentioned in the introduction to Part II, it's best to become an expert in one particular property type, as each type has its own idiosyncrasies: understanding the differences will increase the chances of your success.

Initial information

The first step in due diligence is to get critical information so that you can decide whether to short-list the property and investigate further. If the preliminary checks are positive, you can progress to more detailed due diligence, either before you make an offer or afterward. As discussed in Chapter 15, you may be able to leave it until you have the property under contract, if the contract is subject to inspection and due diligence clauses. However, detailed due diligence must be performed beforehand if you're proposing to buy at auction or are taking a contract without conditions.

Here are some questions to ask the sales agent to assist your initial inquiries. Don't ask them all at once, though, or during your first conversation with the agent, as you might disgruntle them from the start! Also make sure you speak to the property's tenant and find out whatever you can from them first.

Questions to ask the selling agent

- How long has the property been on the market?
- How many offers have you had already?
- Why is the owner selling?
- Is the owner open to part vendor finance?
- Is the owner interested in a short or long settlement?
- Will you be listing similar properties soon?
- Could you please provide some comparable sales?
- Are the tenants paying fair market rent? (Ask the agent to provide some examples to justify their answer here.)
- How long has the tenant been at the premises?
- Is the tenant up to date with rent and outgoings?

- Has the owner ever needed to offer rent abatements (discounts)?

- If there are fewer than two years left on the lease, will the tenant consider exercising their option now (offering rental discounts, if necessary)?

- Could you please provide a depreciation schedule?

- What's the land tax value on the property?

- Who manages the property and how much do they charge?

- Could you give me a copy of the lease, building insurance policy, outgoing statements and rental ledger?

- What developments are happening in the area?

- What's the main source of employment in the area?

CHAPTER NINETEEN

AREA RESEARCH

Understanding the region you're buying in is crucial in detailed due diligence. The region will affect how your property performs in the short and long term in terms of the tenant's success, vacancy rates and capital growth. The aim is to ensure that you always have a profitable tenant.

Understanding the macroeconomics of the area will tell you the long-term growth patterns and which areas will be up and coming with high population growth.

It's not unusual for investors to fear buying in an area they're not familiar with, but modern technology, everything can be researched remotely, so there's no reason not to look in other locations, even interstate. One handy thing to do, especially if you're buying in a different city, is to find someone in the industry (other than the selling agent) with whom you can discuss properties there. Local property managers are useful, as they often have information that's not available to the public – and as the local commercial property industry is surprisingly small, they'll often know the history of a building and its tenant. Be wary of this if a property is listed with multiple agents as such inquiries have a habit of getting back to the selling agent.

In terms of an individual property's location, if you can visit the property, you can learn a lot about it from physically inspecting the building – what the tenants are like, the parking arrangements, foot and road traffic at different times of the day, competition in the area, and how the other tenants get on. Depending on the type of commercial property you buy, you'll need to check different things about the location. For retail, for example, the flow of people at different times of the day and the week is important, and this can help you identify which businesses will flourish.

You probably know that when you're selecting a residential property, quite often the distance to schools, amenities and services is critical. With commercial property, you'll be looking at different types of services and amenities depending on the asset type.

Let's go through the points you should investigate about a property's region and location.

Region research

When researching the region a particular property is in, you want to gather the following information:

- the region's population density and growth
- the current infrastructure and planned future spending
- the location of hospitals, schools and other amenities
- the location of the major shopping and industrial areas
- whether there are areas that could be redeveloped in the future
- whether there's space available to develop similar buildings – lack of such space can reduce vacancy rates in the future and increase demand
- where the region is in the commercial property cycle (as discussed in Chapter 12)

- whether the area is seasonal – in other words, whether it's a tourism destination.

It can be helpful to speak with town planners when doing this research.

Comparable sales and rentals in the area

Obviously, it's important to know how a property compares to others in the area, so:

- Check recent sales and cap rates in the area.
- Check comparable properties' lease lengths.

Remember, as we discussed in Chapter 7, if the tenant is paying below-market rent, an increase is possible at the next rent review. If a tenant is on a short lease and paying below-market rent, this could in fact be an upside if you can buy the property at an equivalent cap rate to the area with the current rent.

Note that in order to compare cap rates, you'll need to check that the property's floor areas match what's been advertised (for retail, check the outdoor area; for industrial, check the mezzanine area).

The property's location

Next, consider the property's location:

- Is access to the building easy?
- Does it have street exposure?
- What signage is there and how visible is it?
- Does the building have good natural light?
- Are the property's storage areas separate from the commercial premises?
- Can the tenant's business expand in the current location?

- Is there a mix of complementary neighbouring businesses to bring foot traffic?

- Is the property in a compatible area? It's often better to be surrounded by buildings with similar uses – many tenants, for example, won't want to lease office space in a building that's next door to a noisy warehouse.

- What are the neighbours like? Be wary of neighbouring businesses that could put off future tenants or increase crime, such as a nightclub or a drug rehab centre.

- Are there anchor tenants to keep the area demand strong?

- How are nearby businesses performing?

Parking

Parking is another important component. Find out:

- What type of parking is there?

- Is it secure?

- Is it free? If not, what's the monthly rate?

- How many exclusive car parks are there for the property?

- Is it a tandem car park (i.e. one car behind the other)? This makes it difficult for the car at the back to get out.

- Are the car parks undercover and underground?

- Is there permitted on-street parking? Is it ticketed?

- What's the car park lighting like? This is especially important if parking is critical to your property and the time of day it's required. If your tenant works late or operates after hours, you want to ensure that the parking areas are well lit and safe at any time of day.

Foot and road traffic

Get a feel for the area at different times of day. Is it well patronised, with heavy foot traffic? This is critical for retail properties.

- Is the building generally attractive (i.e. does it have kerb appeal)?

- Is the property visible from the main street/road?

- What storey is the property on? (second storey retail and restaurants can struggle with performance more than ground floor)

- Is it well landscaped and well maintained?

- How many cars drive past and can see the property for exposure?

- If the area has heavy road traffic is it easy for them to stop and park at the shop location?

- What's the initial impression of the building? If possible, find a building with timeless qualities that will appeal to tenants over the long term.

- Are there transport links close by (e.g. a bus stop or train station)?

- Does the premises have disabled access for wheelchair users and prams?

Vacancy periods

Check the vacancy periods in the area – what's the vacancy rate for the style of property you're looking at? Speak with property managers to ascertain the demand for this style of property and do a historical occupancy study. This can be performed by speaking with a property manager in the region, as well as by using online resources such as CoreLogic to check the property's advertising history. If the risk of vacancy outweighs the long-term net return, don't be tempted by higher net yields.

Also, analyse the competition in the area – other properties where your tenant could move. Ideally, as with the region, there will not be many competing properties in the immediate vicinity and not much land nearby that can be developed into the same type of property; it can be beneficial if the building is in a closely held residential area.

Things to watch out for

When you're researching a property's area and location, these are the red flags:

- It's in a town that only has one or two primary industries supporting it.

- It's in a town with a small population.

- It's a low socio-economic area (however, this is dependent on the tenant – charity shops, fast-food restaurants and so on do well in lower socio-economic areas).

- There are high crime rates.

- The area is seasonal (although this depends on the business and the level of seasonal fluctuation).

- The property has limited visibility.

- It's in a high-competition area.

- There are plenty of available spaces for competitors.

- There's no parking (unless the property is in a CBD area where this is common and not so much of a disadvantage).

- There's low foot or road traffic.

Zoning and overlays

Zoning and overlays are the next aspect of a property's location to consider. In Australia, all land has a designated zone type that permits certain kinds of activity. There are generally four zones – residential, commercial, industrial and agricultural – and an area can also be classified as mixed use. Within a zone, there are often definitions of the types of commercial and industrial businesses that can be carried out and requirements about points such as building heights.

Zoning can sometimes determine if you're allowed to change the exterior of a shopfront, put advertising signs on the building, change its internal fit-out, put telecommunication devices (mobile phone towers and/or satellite dishes) on top of the building, or use outdoor seating or heaters on a footpath. Zoning and planning issues dictate the use and development of areas, and hence affect the property's value.

Note that areas which are designated as low-density are less likely to have mass development in the future compared to areas where medium- and high-rises are permitted. This has two sides: oversupply is less likely to occur, as developers usually consider it too expensive to buy out a number of properties to then build only a few storeys high, but the investor is unable to develop their property for profit.

Local councils are responsible for deciding what zoning is appropriate and ensuring businesses and properties comply with their regulations. So, anyone buying commercial property, or planning to change or modify a commercial property, needs to contact the local council to see what's possible and what plans and permits they'll need. Local council town planners are an excellent source of information here and should be consulted before a commercial purchase.

Planning overlays are local government controls for specific pieces of land, and include items such as flood zones, bushfire risk, noise corridors, heritage listings, transport noise, landslide risk and airport noise. You can find out about these on the relevant local government area (LGA) website and assess the risk and applicability to your property.

Specific things to check:

- the type of zoning

- whether the property is zoned for current and future tenant use

- if the property has heritage listing

- future zoning potential (if there are value-add opportunities down the track with zoning changes)

- the zoning of the surrounding area

- easements (a section of land registered on your property's title, which gives someone the right to use the land for a specific purpose even though they're not the land owner – examples include shared driveways, right of access, right to light and air, and services such as gas and drainage lines)

- the density of the area.

CHAPTER TWENTY

TENANT AND BUSINESS ANALYSIS

A commercial property's tenant is critical to the investment's profitability. Analysing the tenant and their business will help you determine the longevity of their business, and the likelihood that they will take up lease options when it's time to renew.

Tenant analysis

As mentioned in Chapter 18, speaking with the tenant before you talk to the real estate agent is a good idea, at it helps you to get an accurate picture of the situation. The agent cannot tell you not to contact a tenant – be wary if an agent wants you to sign a non-disclosure agreement (NDA) which prevents you speaking to the tenant. This could occur simply because the owner does not want the tenant to know about the sale, or it could be for unethical reasons.

The following questions will help you gauge the longevity of the area and the tenant:

- Have you been told the property is for sale?
- Is your business doing well?

- Have you considered buying the building yourself?
- Who owns the business?
- How long have you been there?
- How many staff do you have?
- Are there any rent abatements (discounts applied during slow periods of trade)?
- Does the business have multiple locations?
- Where do you want your business to be or what do you want it to look like in the next 10 years?
- Would you sign a longer lease if I bought the property? (This will indicate the tenant's commitment and give them some assurance they won't be evicted.)
- At what times do you do most of your business?
- Are there any outstanding issues or maintenance problems?
- Are there any things you'd like to do to this property or the complex?
- What's your relationship like with the strata management? (If applicable.)
- What's your relationship like with the nearby tenants?
- Do you have there any main competitors nearby?
- Do you see any future issues with your industry?
- What demographic of people usually comes to these premises?
- How do most customers get to your premises?
- Is there enough parking?
- Are there any other available properties that are similar to this?
- How long have the other tenants been here, do you know?
- Who owns the fit-out? (Banks don't usually include the fit-outs in their valuations.)

Depending on the tenant's industry, they may be required to have licences and permits – a common type of permit is for the food and beverage industry, which requires equipment such as deep-fryers. The local council must approve their use and it this should be checked. A lease will usually outline the permitted use of the premises – you should ensure that the tenant is allowed to do the activities required for their business, including providing all the types of goods and services they offer. In the lease, never guarantee the permitted use of the property: make sure the tenant is responsible for use and approvals.

Note that, as mentioned earlier in the book, it is possible to negotiate an 'agreement to lease' with the tenant during the due diligence process. This may mean a small rent reduction or changing a 3 per cent rental increase to CPI; however, it's a small price to pay because it helps with finance and valuations. You'll be able to readjust the rent at the end of the lease period.

Business analysis

In buying a commercial property that's tenanted, you are in effect buying into the tenant's business and its future. Your analysis of the business should cover the following:

- How busy is the business?

- What competition is there in the area?

- How long has the business been running? Ideally, you're looking for a tenant who has been in the property for more than five years – their business will be more established and past the typical period of three years in which most businesses fail.

- Who runs the business and how many staff are there? Beware of businesses that are dependent on one person, as if they leave the business, it could fail.

- Is the business owner the occupier? They often show more care, because their personal wealth depends on success. Investors in businesses, by comparison, show less care and are less loyal to the location.

- Are big national tenants moving to the area? This can be a solid indicator of growth. These companies can spend millions of dollars in research for their locations, as a failed location can cost the company an exorbitant amount of money due to the large startup costs. However, would a big national tenant moving to the area be detrimental to the business?

As well as the business's current status, it's also important to understand possible future industries in the area. Technology has created but is also destroying many businesses – video rental shops, for example, were wiped out by streaming services. The same applies to gaming stores. The shift online means that many types of retail stores are shutting, and others are struggling. For example, newsagencies are still around, but sales of lottery tickets, magazines, newspapers and birthday cards are declining, so they'll need to evolve. Petrol stations may also have a shorter future because of the increasing popularity of electric cars.

Some service-based businesses such as electronic repair or computer shops have shut because, with the falling price of electronics, it's no longer economical to repair things, and branded companies are looking after their own servicing.

The coronavirus pandemic, of course, has changed the way many businesses operate – temporarily or permanently, it remains to be seen.

Lease review

As a formal part of the due diligence into the tenant and business, it's advisable to have a solicitor review the lease.

Be aware that even if you have a copy of the lease, informal arrangements can be made between the owner and tenant as well, so it's a good idea to inspect at least 12 months of rental history. You can do this by obtaining a rental ledger from the property manager or owner, which will show you actual income, when it was paid, and any late payments or rental concessions. Concessions – such as rent-free periods or rental reductions – aren't necessarily stipulated in the lease, and so can be hidden. Concessions are usually provided when a tenant is struggling financially, or in return for the tenant carrying out renovations from which the owner will benefit.

Be wary of leasebacks. A leaseback is a financial arrangement in which the owner of a property sells it to an investor, who at the same time leases the property back to the seller, thus freeing up the original owner's capital while still allowing them to use the property. You'll need to investigate their reason for selling: more often than not, they simply want to sell the property with a lease in place (thus achieving a higher sales price) but have plans to move in the future. There are legitimate reasons for a seller doing a lease-back, however, such as trying to expand the business, or incurring unexpected personal costs.

We discussed leases in detail in Chapter 7. The key areas to focus on during due diligence are:

- lessee details – leases can be in the name of trusts or companies that can remove assets and close easily, which reduces your security
- rent review stipulations
- financial security – this involves checking all guarantees. A personal guarantee is preferable, but check that the guarantor has assets, preferable a property that cannot be easily sold.
- fit-out and make-good clauses
- repairs and maintenance clauses

- assignment and subleasing details
- tax information
- any special conditions.

Body corporate review

If you're buying a strata-titled commercial property, obtaining a physical body corporate records report is recommended, as there can be many service contracts in effect, especially in a large complex. This is a physical inspection of the body corporate records. It will point out any special or unusual levies, potential future expenditure, and so on. The body corporate is usually responsible for preparing these reports.

They usually cost $300 to $1000 and will typically go through the past three years' records to identify any issues with the specific property lot or common property. The report should also verify the figures given by the selling agent on strata levies.

The key items to take note of in a body corporate report are as follows:

- **Financial position.** Body corporates don't trade or invest – their only source of funding is the levy paid by each of the lot owners. The report will provide details of the administration and sinking funds, which will show you how healthy the surplus is for the size of the building, or if there are any arrears. It will also note any big future expenses or levies that would be required on the property.

- **Building defects.** All buildings have some form of defect. It's usually minor and cosmetic, but some buildings have major structural defects that affect the tenants' enjoyment of their property and become a major financial drain. It's vital to be aware of any already discovered defects on the common property. The report can show regular maintenance issues that are problematic.

- **Disputes.** Body corporates often have disputes – between fellow lot owners, with the strata committee, with the property management, with contractors and with other parties. Mostly these disputes are minor, but sometimes they become devastating for the entire body corporate and lead to major financial losses.

- **Compliance with legislation.** Legislation on body corporates is complex and far-reaching, and non-compliance can lead to significant problems and losses.

- **Management issues.** Body corporate management is a complex interchange between a third-party company and the owners, and there can be breakdowns in communication and leadership issues. Infighting is not uncommon, nor is lack of any leadership at all. Poor management leads to an inability to resolve other issues, so it's particularly important.

- **Certificate of currency.** A certificate of currency is issued by your insurance provider to confirm that the insurance policy on the property is effective and valid. It usually specifies the conditions of the insurance, including the policy type held, the premium paid and the date the policy expires. It's essential that your property is insured for the correct amount to avoid penalties for underinsurance in the instance of a claim. For instance, if you were to insure the building for 80 per cent of the property's replacement value, the insurer would give you only 80 per cent of your insured value (not the replacement value) in the event of damage, because it's insuring the percentage of risk. You need to ensure that the property is adequately insured for more than or equal to the replacement value to avoid losses should anything occur. It's also worth checking the insurance cover for specific perils such as bushfire, landslide and hail, as they're not always included as standard. The public liability limit should also be appropriate for the exposure related to the occupancy of the building. A certificate of currency will usually be required to obtain finance.

CHAPTER TWENTY-ONE
BUILDING AND PEST INSPECTIONS

It should go without saying that it's important to inspect the physical building to see the quality of the construction, its condition, and its susceptibility to pests. When inspecting, take time to discover if there are any potential issues that could arise, especially ones that may be seasonal or intermittent, which the building and pest inspector may not be aware of. Some examples include poor drainage of the common areas during heavy rain periods, mould issues due to poor light and ventilation, cracking due to heat, and inadequate heating or cooling.

It's advisable to take lots of photos and videos inside and outside, so you have a reference if an issue arises with a tenant in the future. Make sure you view the whole building, no matter how much inconvenience it may cause to the tenant. This includes storage rooms and parking.

Here are some key things to look for:

- What type of exterior does the building have? How will it look in 10 years' time when leases expire and you may want to sell or release the building?

- What's the proportion of lifts to floor area? It's often recommended that you have one lift per 3000 square metres. The speeds of lifts is also important, as people don't like to be kept waiting.

- If it's an industrial property, what's the ratio of floor space to mezzanine area to office area? Is this suitable for the area and tenants it's looking to service?

- What amenities does the building have? Larger buildings often have a fitness centre, a café, communal conference rooms or small retail outlets. Smaller office buildings typically don't have these amenities, but similar facilities should be located nearby.

- Does the building have facilities for disabled access?

- Is the lobby or entrance area modern-looking or outdated, and is the image it presents appropriate to the types of tenants you want to attract? Note that many firms are conscious of cost issues and don't want extravagant foyers.

- Is the selling agent's description of the floor space accurate when compared with the physical building? The best way to establish this is to have a building inspector measure the floor space. Discrepancies may be due to the sales agent getting the figure wrong or the building not having been built according to the original plans. If there is a discrepancy, you should ask to see the building drawings and also the 'as-built' drawings. In warehouses, a mezzanine area is quite often included as part of the warehouse floor space. In retail properties, it's common to include the outdoor seating area as part of the floor space. You need to verify the area of each type of floor space and compare this with the rental rates.

- Are there signs of poor maintenance, such as poor landscaping, dirty surfaces or peeling paint? Some owners will cut back on repairs and maintenance when they plan to sell the property, and/or do cover-up jobs or low-quality maintenance. If a seller or tenant has cut back on maintenance over a long period, this can indicate that the short-term outlook for the property isn't good.

- Is there asbestos in the building? An asbestos report is recommended if there's any evidence it may be present – asbestos can be extremely expensive to remove, because it's so dangerous when disturbed. Sometimes the seller will agree to provide such a report at their own cost. In some cases, the seller will have to include a statement in the transfer documents that the building has no known asbestos. If the property contains asbestos, the maintenance cost or future removal costs need to be budgeted for.

It's important to request all service contracts for the building; a good building manager should have them to hand. These can indicate whether any big maintenance procedures or equipment replacements are coming up. You should also ask whether any work is planned to comply with council, fire or other regulations and if there are quotes for this work. Information such as this can be a useful negotiating tool.

After the initial inspection of the property, the next step is to have a qualified building and pest inspector formally inspect the building. These inspections can be performed once the property is under contract if there's a building and pest clause or a due diligence clause in the contract. It's essential the inspector is experienced, because anything missed can be very expensive. An experienced inspector will also be able to give you estimates of how much items will cost to be fixed. It is worth noting that the inspectors do not guarantee the quality of the property: they only report on their findings.

Building and pest inspectors usually charge between $500 and $1,400 for a standard inspection. Even if you're an experienced builder and renovator, having a third-party inspection can be helpful in negotiations, as the inspector's report will bear more weight than your observations. It's best to book the inspection towards the end of the due diligence process, so you don't incur that cost if you don't go ahead with the purchase for other reasons. Most building inspectors will also perform pest inspections.

CHAPTER TWENTY-TWO

DUE DILIGENCE CHECKLIST

This chapter provides a list I personally use when conducting due diligence for my clients and personal properties. It's a very extensive list, but not all items need to be addressed, as it will depend on the asset type, location and complicity of the deal.

Due diligence can take anywhere from a day to over a week, as it's on how many variables there are with the property. If you're time-poor or uncomfortable performing this due diligence, it may be best to utilise the services of a credible commercial buyer's agent.

Property information

Site

☐ Site plan
☐ Floor plans
☐ As-built diagrams of the building
☐ Parking schedules
☐ Recent land tax assessment notice
☐ Inventory list
☐ Council documents
☐ Existing management agreements
☐ Certificate of currency/building insurance certificate

- [ ] Body corporate report
- [ ] Title reference for property and title search
- [ ] Details of easements, covenants, restrictions on use or encroachments affecting the property
- [ ] Drainage and sewerage diagrams showing current connections
- [ ] Details of shared access or any right-of-way arrangements

Occupational health and safety

- [ ] Hazardous materials register and reports
- [ ] Details of any hazardous materials stored on site
- [ ] Details of any hazardous materials used in the construction of the property

Service contracts

- [ ] Roof maintenance
- [ ] Air conditioning maintenance
- [ ] Lift or escalator maintenance
- [ ] Interior plants maintenance
- [ ] Outdoor landscaping
- [ ] Cleaning maintenance
- [ ] Hazardous waste removal
- [ ] Rubbish removal
- [ ] Parking contracts
- [ ] Property-management contracts
- [ ] Security contracts
- [ ] Utilities contracts

Value-add opportunities

- [ ] Changing its use
- [ ] Raising rents
- [ ] Improving the property's quality and image
- [ ] Creating new sources of revenue
- [ ] Marketing the property

- ☐ Removing underperforming tenants
- ☐ Better property management
- ☐ Development

Area research

- ☐ Comparable sales
- ☐ Comparable rents
- ☐ Foot and road traffic analysis
- ☐ Historical occupancy study
- ☐ Vacancy periods

Council and town planning

- ☐ Council development consents and conditions
- ☐ Construction certificates
- ☐ Final occupation certificates
- ☐ Building certificates
- ☐ Fire safety certificates
- ☐ Heritage listing
- ☐ Conservation

Zoning

- ☐ Type of zoning
- ☐ Future zoning potential
- ☐ Information from town planner

Tenant and business analysis

Documents

- ☐ Rental ledgers or evidence for at least 12 months
- ☐ Tenant's financial statements
- ☐ Proof of payment of outgoings and utility bills
- ☐ Identity check of business owner
- ☐ Credit check on owner and business

☐ Evidence of assets
☐ Reference of tenant from previous landlords

Business information
☐ Age of business
☐ Previous locations
☐ How long the business has operated at current location
☐ Whether the business owners know the property is for sale
☐ Whether the tenants have considered buying the property themselves
☐ Whether the business owners appear professional
☐ Owner's previous business experience
☐ Whether the business is doing well
☐ The number of staff in the business
☐ Whether there are multiple shops and locations
☐ The area that the business services
☐ Business competition in the area
☐ How the tenant sees their business in 10 years
☐ The usual operating times
☐ Outstanding issues or maintenance
☐ Anything the business would like to do to the property or the complex
☐ Relationship with the body corporate
☐ Relationship with the other tenants
☐ Any foreseeable issues with their industry
☐ What demographic usually comes to the property
☐ How most customers get to the property
☐ Whether there's enough parking
☐ Whether there are other properties available similar to this
☐ How long the neighbouring tenants have been there
☐ Whether the tenant can provide suppliers' references

Lease review

Documents

- ☐ Lease
- ☐ Amendments to leases
- ☐ Subleases
- ☐ Rental abatements
- ☐ Licenses, insurances, permits and development approvals for tenants' business
- ☐ Car parking arrangements
- ☐ Bank guarantees, personal guarantees and lease securities
- ☐ List of owner's fixtures and fittings being sold
- ☐ Evidence of payment by vendor for any tenant's fixtures
- ☐ List of tenant's fixtures and fittings
- ☐ Depreciation schedule

Lease details

- ☐ Lease start and end dates
- ☐ Lease term and length
- ☐ Renewal and expansion options
- ☐ Whether lessee is under a personal name or a company

Rent review

- ☐ Annual rent review method
- ☐ Any ratchet clauses (clauses that stop rent reductions after reviews)
- ☐ Verification of whether the rent paid matches the lease

Security

- ☐ Are there bank and personal guarantees and bonds?
- ☐ Are the guarantees and bond of sufficient value?
- ☐ Does the bond increase each year with rental rises?
- ☐ Verify all securities such as personal and bank guarantees

Fit-out and make-good clauses

- ☐ Who owns the fit-out in the property?
- ☐ Are there tenant improvement allowances for things such as renovations or refurbishment?
- ☐ Who's responsible for maintenance of the fit-out?
- ☐ Who's responsible for removal of the fit-out at the end of the lease?
- ☐ Are there regular redecoration clauses?
- ☐ What's the period for any redecoration clauses?

Insurances

- ☐ What insurance policies does the tenant hold? (e.g. public liability cover)

Outgoings

- ☐ List of recoverable outgoings
- ☐ Percentage of building's outgoings recovered from tenant
- ☐ Verification of payment by tenant of outgoings
- ☐ Whether land tax and property management are recoverable

Repairs and maintenance

- ☐ Who's responsible for general repairs and maintenance?
- ☐ Who's responsible for specific items such as the building structure, pest control and cleaning?

Assignment and subleasing

- ☐ Are there any subleasing agreements?
- ☐ Is the consent of the landlord required for these?

Tax

- ☐ Does the tenant pay the GST component of the rent?

Special conditions

- ☐ Are there nominated car parks?

- ☐ Are there any undocumented incentives?
- ☐ Do they need to be formally documented?
- ☐ Have there been any rental concessions such as reduced rent or a free month's rent?
- ☐ What's in the cancellation and termination clauses?
- ☐ Are there any additional expenses or duties?
- ☐ Are there any special building allowances?
- ☐ Are there demolition clauses (to enable the landlord to demolish the property at a specified time)?
- ☐ Are there 'make good the condition of the property' provisions?

Building and pest inspection

Documents

- ☐ Builder's details and date of construction
- ☐ Evidence of builder's warranty and defect liability insurance
- ☐ History of claims against builder
- ☐ Engineering certification for concrete slabs (including load-bearing capacity for industrial properties)
- ☐ Council-approved plans and specifications
- ☐ Records of any work undertaken in past five years

Photos and videos

- ☐ Outside the property
- ☐ Nearby properties
- ☐ Inside the building
- ☐ Any noticeable improvements
- ☐ Any potential value-add opportunities

External condition and materials

- ☐ Driveway
- ☐ Paths/paved areas
- ☐ Roller door sizes

- ☐ Space to manoeuvre vehicles
- ☐ Fire compliance
- ☐ External roof:
  - ☐ Flashings
  - ☐ Gutters and downpipes
  - ☐ Valleys
- ☐ Eaves and bargeboards
- ☐ Roof interior:
  - ☐ Roof framing
  - ☐ Roof supports
  - ☐ Insulation and sarking
- ☐ Windows
- ☐ Subfloor
- ☐ Footings
- ☐ External walls
- ☐ Weepholes and vents
- ☐ Damp course
- ☐ External stairs
- ☐ Balcony
- ☐ Veranda
- ☐ Fences and gates
- ☐ Retaining walls
- ☐ Paths/paved areas
- ☐ Landscaping
- ☐ Site drainage
- ☐ Parking

Services

- ☐ Land capacity of utilities
- ☐ Emergency generator
- ☐ Lifts
- ☐ Water lines and pressure
- ☐ Piping

- ☐ Pumps
- ☐ Hot-water system

Internal condition

- ☐ Ceiling condition
- ☐ Walls
- ☐ Doors
- ☐ Floors
- ☐ Woodwork
- ☐ Furnishings
- ☐ Kitchen
- ☐ Kitchen fixtures
- ☐ Kitchen tiles
- ☐ Bathrooms
- ☐ Bathroom fixtures
- ☐ Bathroom tiles
- ☐ Toilets
- ☐ Toilet fixtures
- ☐ Toilet ventilation
- ☐ Stairs internal
- ☐ Ceiling height for usage
- ☐ Sprinkler heights

Pest inspection

- ☐ Timber pest check
- ☐ Termites
- ☐ Borers
- ☐ Wood decay or fungi
- ☐ Moisture issues
- ☐ Susceptibility to pests

PART VI
CONVEYANCING, FINANCE AND BUYING STRUCTURES

Now let's go on to look at the legal and financial aspects of commercial property purchases. Conveyancing, choosing and obtaining finance and deciding on an ownership structure for your investments require careful consideration if you're to achieve the best possible investment outcome. We'll explore these topics in turn in the chapters this part of the book.

CHAPTER TWENTY-THREE

CONVEYANCING

The main purpose of the conveyancing process is to transfer the legal title or ownership of the property from one party to another. The process usually starts from the time you enter into your contract (the date of the contract) and continues through to the settlement of the purchase. The conveyancing work is performed by a solicitor or conveyancer; a solicitor is a legally trained professional, while a conveyancer has been taught conveyancing but isn't legally trained.

The solicitor or conveyancer you choose needs to be well versed in the laws of the state in which they work, as there are many differences among the states. Look for someone who's highly experienced, not just the person with the cheapest rates. The settlement process can be messy so you need someone who's confident and will have your best interests at heart.

Once you and the seller have agreed on all the terms of the contract and have signed it, the contract will be dated on the date the last person signed. This is known as 'exchanging contracts' or the property being 'under contract', depending on the state of Australia. The contract is legally binding after it's been signed by both parties. The deposit is usually paid before the buyer signs, but in some states (such as Queensland) it can be done after signing, as specified in the contract. The amount of deposit is negotiated between the parties through the sales agent and is paid to the agent as the stakeholder either on signing, or on another date as agreed between the parties.

The contract will contain conditions that you the buyer needs to satisfy, including due diligence, finance approval and building and pest inspections. The period between the signing of the contract and satisfaction of these clauses is known as 'conditional'; once the clauses are satisfied, the contract becomes 'unconditional' and the buyer and seller must proceed to settlement.

During the due diligence period, your solicitor or conveyancer will undertake pre-purchase searches and enquiries. These include checks with government and non-government authorities to ensure there are no outstanding interests or problems with the property. Some of these searches can be performed after the contract is unconditional if they will not affect the outcome of the sale.

The list of searches that can be undertaken is extensive, so it's best to discuss with your solicitor or conveyancer which are appropriate for your transaction because the costs can add up quickly. The most common are:

- title search

- registered plan

- local authority rates search

- special water-meter reading

- land tax search

- transport and main roads search

- priority notice, if required.

Your solicitor can also arrange an inspection of the body corporate records (also known as a strata report), but many other companies can do this work. In New South Wales, this report should be obtained before going under contract.

Once the contract becomes unconditional, a settlement date is booked with all parties (including any outgoing or incoming lenders). Before settlement day, any special conditions such as repairs or removal of items left at the property must be satisfied – this is usually done through a pre-settlement inspection, which most commercial investors will get their property manager to do.

For settlement to occur, all parties, including the banks, must be ready to settle. Transfer documents must be signed and returned and stamp duty paid if it's a paper settlement, or all matters completed on PEXA, the e-conveyance platform, for Property Exchange Australia. The parties' respective solicitors or conveyancers will prepare the transfer documents, arrange for the seller to organise the release of mortgage (if there is one) and liaise with the banks to prepare for settlement.

Before settlement the solicitors/conveyancers will ensure all documents have been prepared and executed correctly, that settlement figures have been adjusted accurately, and everything necessary has been completed.

On settlement day, the parties' solicitors or conveyancers and their bank representatives will be present for the buyer to pay the balance of the purchase price in exchange for the title transfer and release of the mortgage. If the seller has a mortgage, the seller will give their bank's representative a cheque (or certified electronic transfer) to pay out this mortgage in exchange for its release.

After settlement, the solicitor or conveyancer will contact the seller's real estate agent, authorising the release of the keys to the buyer and the deposit to the seller.

If the buyer has obtained finance from a lender, the lender will attend to the registration of the transfer, the release of mortgage (if any) and registration of the buyer's mortgage at the Land Registry Services. If the property is being bought with cash, the buyer's solicitor will attend to the registration of the requisite documents. If the transaction was performed through PEXA, payment of the purchase price and registration of the transfer, release of the seller's mortgage and registration of the buyer's mortgage will occur immediately online.

Once settlement has occurred, the buyer becomes the legal owner of the property and the seller is released from any further obligations for payment of rates or taxes – these become the buyer's responsibility. The lender will usually hold the title of the property until the loan is paid off.

CHAPTER TWENTY-FOUR
FINANCE

Finance is such an important piece of the commercial investing puzzle. Without a thorough understanding of it, or without obtaining advice from a qualified adviser with the appropriate expertise, it will be difficult to expand your portfolio.

Lenders will generally finance a residential property based on the contract price, assuming you haven't bought greatly above market value.

Unlike residential property, commercial properties require a third-party formal, in-depth valuation that considers many of the items in the 'Due Diligence' section of this book. Lenders will normally lend on the lesser of the two between the valuation or purchase price figure; some will use the contract of sale as a valuation as long as certain conditions are met.

In any case, when you're looking to buy a commercial property it's best to think like a lender, as this will help with your forecasting, strategy and value-adding possibilities to extract equity. Lenders constantly change their criteria for lending, but will always look well on a low-risk property that's positively geared – meaning that you earn more from rent than your loan repayments. Commercial lenders will look at the quality of the property and then your personal circumstances.

It's important not to fear 'good debt', although you should be cautious about 'bad debt':

- **Bad debt** is car loans, credit cards, home loans against owner-occupied properties (these can be a good investment, but they're considered a liability for lending), and debt against liabilities that depreciate.

- **Good debt** is debt against property, investments, collectables or assets that appreciate in value.

You might obtain loans from banks and loan institutions, money partners, joint ventures, or family members. Much like negotiating a property price, it's possible to negotiate loans. There are typically three options when obtaining finance for a commercial property:

1. You could obtain finance from a lender with whom you have already done business.

2. You could investigate the mortgage market on your own.

3. You could engage a commercial broker to investigate the market for you.

1. Using an existing lender

Most people who obtain finance from an existing lender do so for one of two reasons: either they trust and are loyal to their existing lender, or they want to avoid the paperwork involved in going somewhere else for a loan. This method is advisable only if the existing lender is giving you a competitive rate. If you're going to lose thousands of dollars, it's worth reassessing your loyalty!

You won't know if you have the best rate if you don't compare rates from different lenders. A broker will usually be able to tell you quickly if there are more competitive rates, so it's definitely worth at least speaking to one. Sometimes, they'll even suggest that you negotiate a lower rate with your existing lender.

Going with an existing lender can also cap your borrowing, because it rules out second-tier lenders (smaller banks or non-bank lenders).

2. Investigating on your own

Investigating your finance options takes quite a lot of knowledge and time. You need to know each lender's servicing criteria, fees, offers and conditions, and you'll normally need the details of a sample property or the one you're buying to find out what each lender will offer. You then need to submit applications with all the necessary documents and follow the transaction through.

3. Engaging a mortgage broker

Mortgage brokers will compare multiple lenders for you and find the most competitive rates and conditions. Obtaining a loan this way takes much less time and effort than investigating on your own and ensures that you're aware of the variety of options to choose from.

Mortgage brokers

A mortgage broker's job is to work through the types of loans, features and options available to you, and he or she will go direct to multiple lenders and assess the criteria from each institution. These criteria can relate to your ability to service the loan, the interest rate, the loan term and fees, principal and interest loans versus interest-only loans, and the use of offset accounts. The broker will help you compare and choose the right loan for your circumstances and future plans; he or she will also advocate for you if things go wrong with a lender or mortgage application. The broker will work with major banks and non-bank lenders, depending which suits your needs, and find you the best rate. But in the end, it's your decision which lender to go with.

Another big advantage of using a mortgage broker is that they will guide you through the loan application process. However, not all mortgage brokers are trustworthy or competent, and bear in mind that most residential brokers aren't proficient at commercial lending, which has a different range of loan options.

Most people engage a commercial mortgage broker because they do all the work for you and don't charge you – they're paid by the lender once a loan is obtained. Their service is usually uncompromised, nonetheless, as most lenders will pay the broker a similar amount. With commercial finance, the commission most lenders pay to the broker is directly linked to the establishment fee charged for a commercial loan. So, if a lender charges 0.75 per cent of the loan amount as an establishment fee, the broker may get paid 0.5 per cent, with bank therefore making 0.25 per cent. If, for a tight deal, the establishment fee is waived, this may mean that the broker has to forego their upfront commission or reduce it to win the business.

A broker will typically look at more than 20 lenders, which individual investors usually don't have the skills or time to do. As they don't get paid unless they obtain a loan for you, in effect, all this upfront work is unpaid. This motivates them to find the best offer for you. Once you have the offer, you can check websites to see if it's competitive.

Note that you should engage a broker as soon as possible as finance is a lengthy process. It's best to use only one, reputable broker, as you don't want them stepping on each other's toes; also, if a lender has enquiries from two brokers about the same property, it can raise red flags. Once you find a good broker, it's worth being loyal to them to achieve a good long-term outcome.

So, how do you find a good broker? Using the techniques outlined in the 'Build your team' section of Chapter 14, once you have a few names, meet with them and ask the following questions. Consider their answers and check the references they provide, then make your choice.

Questions for mortgage brokers

- What are your qualifications?

- How long have you been a broker?

- How many commercial loans have you sourced?

- How many lenders do you have access to?

- What makes you choose one lender over another?

- Do you have three recent clients you can provide as a reference?

Loan to value ratio

We've touched on loan to value ratio (LVR) earlier in the book – it represents what percentage of your own money (i.e. your deposit) is required in relation to a property's purchase price. This is another factor when selecting a lender.

As mentioned previously, commercial property loans require a larger deposit due to the higher risk associated, the longer periods of vacancy and the time spent selling – typically, you'll need at least a 30 per cent deposit, meaning a 70 per cent LVR. So, if you were to buy a $1 million commercial property on a 70 per cent LVR, for example, you'd need to give the bank $300,000 to obtain the loan. In addition to paying interest on the $700,000 debt, you'll need capital for costs such as stamp duty, legal fees, building and pest inspections, and valuations. These can amount to roughly 5 per cent of the purchase price. (We looked at purchasing costs in detail in Chapter 5.)

You could find a lender that offers a lower interest rate, but requires a 65 per cent LVR. So you need to assess where your money is best spent and what your goals and requirements are. Having a larger LVR will usually enable you to borrow more and expand your portfolio more quickly.

CHAPTER TWENTY-FIVE
TYPES OF LENDERS AND LOANS

Commercial property loan terms are generally shorter than those of residential loans: they will usually be 15 to 25 years, although there are some lenders offering up to 30 years. The average actual duration is three to four years, because most investors will refinance the property to release equity, obtain a better rate or to buy more property. For properties such as shopping centres, lenders will typically take 75 per cent of the WALE as the loan term. For instance, if you had a four-year WALE, the lenders would give you a three-year loan. At the end of the three years, you will incur more bank fees as another application will be necessary. Hence, it's favourable to have as long a WALE as possible.

In this chapter, we'll look more closely the different types of lenders and loans to choose from.

Types of lenders

There's a large landscape of lenders to choose from when obtaining finance for a commercial property, but they can differ dramatically in the way they operate. Let's run through the three main types now: major banks, mutuals and private funders.

Major banks

Major banks are the most common type of lender and the type with which most people are familiar. They offer the advantage of a big branch network, though internet banking has made this less important for many people. Banks are generally owned by shareholders and are usually listed on the stock exchange.

Mutuals

Building societies and credit unions fall under the banner of 'mutuals', as they are owned by members, not shareholders. The major difference between credit unions and building societies on the one hand and banks on the other is that with mutuals, the profits are reinvested for the members – whereas with banks, the profits are for the benefit of their shareholders. Members of mutuals own their credit union or building society, whereas customers of banks are not shareholders. Members of a mutual may therefore benefit from enhanced services, and lower interest rates and fees in some instances. Most mutuals clients feel a sense of loyalty towards building societies and credit unions because they receive more personalised attention.

Mutuals offer a range of financial services and products, including home loans, personal and car loans, credit cards, and savings and everyday transactional accounts. Although they have a different ownership structure to that of a conventional bank, they are still authorised deposit-taking institutions and are regulated by the Australian Prudential Regulation Authority (APRA) to the same extent the banks are.

Private funders

Private funders (or lenders) are often a conglomerate of wealthy people who pool their money to lend funds at premium rates. Private lenders often have a greater risk appetite; however, this generally means high interest rates and establishment fees. These lenders will be more focused on security than your ability to service the loan, and more interested in the quality of the property and tenant when determining the loan amount.

Private funders are usually lenders of last resort because their fees are high, but they are a fast-growing avenue for developers and investors. Because their loans are not covered by the *National Consumer Credit Protection Act*, they can be a lot easier and faster to obtain.

Types of loans

How you structure the finance on your commercial properties is one of the most important parts of your investment strategy. There's an abundance of loan products available, but note that commercial and residential property loans are different. Residential loans are usually principal and interest (P&I) or interest-only (IO) and are over 20 to 30 years. Commercial loans have more variety and will usually be the length of the lease or 10 to 20 years.

The fees attached to commercial property loans can vary wildly, so it's important to check these before taking on a loan. A low interest rate may not be cheaper than a higher rate with lower fees.

Before you approach a lender, you should stress-test the whole deal and consider how you would manage if interest rates go up. Many lenders apply a 2.5 per cent increase on your presented interest rate, so this is usually a good starting point to stress-test. Depending on your risk profile, this is what may help you decide whether to go fixed or variable interest rates. It will also depend on what your exit strategy is, or if you were required to sell the property urgently.

There are a number of different types of commercial loans, including full documentation, no documentation and lease documentation loans; lines of credit; and split loans. Refinancing, using commercial bills and vendor finance are other options. Let's look at each of these now.

Fixed vs variable interest rates

On most loan types, lenders may offer loans with fixed interest rates or variable rates, which we've touched on before:

- **A fixed rate** enables you to lock in your interest rate (and therefore your loan repayments) for a set period, usually one to five years. During this time, your interest rate will remain the same, regardless of any changes to the official cash rate. The rate of a fixed-rate loan will be higher than that for a variable loan at the time you take up the loan, but if interest rates rise, you'll be financially better off. When the fixed term ends, the interest rate reverts to a variable rate. If you pay out the fixed rate early there may be financial penalties from the lender.

- **Variable rates** are the most flexible; loans with variable rates generally allow you to make extra repayments and also to redraw on the repayments. If interest rates go up, however, you may be in a worse position than if you had a fixed rate.

Principal and interest vs interest-only loans

Principal and interest (P&I) loans are the most common type for everyday investors. With these loans, you gradually reduce the amount of money you owe by paying off a portion of the principal each month. The monthly repayment is thus higher than it would be for an equivalent interest-only loan.

Interest-only loans, however, are the most popular for commercial property investors, as they're more tax-effective and will increase a portfolio's cash flow due to the lower repayments. No principal is paid off the loan during the loan term – which is usually three to five years – only the interest on the borrowings. Once the loan's term is completed, it will revert to a principal and interest loan, unless the property is refinanced.

Full documentation loans

The full documentation or 'full doc' loan is the most common type of mortgage issued by Australian lenders. You will have to provide more information for this than for any other loan application, including details of your income, asset base, outgoings and your debts.

No documentation and low documentation loans

If you're self-employed, a contractor, or even a professional investor, it's usually more difficult to provide all the financial documents to satisfy the lender's requirements. 'No doc' or 'low doc' loans were very popular before the global financial crisis of 2008–09 but are now less common. They require less information about your assets and liabilities, but the rules are more relaxed compared with a full doc loan. The lender will mitigate this risk by requiring a larger deposit (usually minimum 35 per cent) and require a higher rate.

No doc and low doc loans aren't normally designed to be in place for a long period of time: they will have a term of six months to three years and then their interest rate will increase. The lenders want to know you have an exit plan to repay the loan.

Lease documentation loans

Lease documentation loans are excellent for investors who have several properties and cash and are reaching the limit of their loan serviceability – meaning that lenders consider them unable to service another loan with their personal income (from employment or from assets owned outright). For a lease-doc loan, lenders solely look at the asset and the tenant involved to determine a borrowing amount based on the property's net income.

Lease doc loans can be useful for:

- people who have an extensive property portfolio and would find it difficult to get a loan under full doc arrangements, and

- people in a syndicate or with a complex corporate tree who are unable to trace the flow of money.

Most lease doc loans are used for new acquisitions, so the lender knows that the buyer isn't relying on that income to cover other debts. The lease on the property generally needs to be a registered lease (one that's registered with the relevant state body) – or one being negotiated with the expectation that it will be registered to an unrelated third party. The specific criteria for the loan, which will vary from lender to lender, will be about minimum interest cover requirements. The loan term will usually be in line with the remaining lease term (excluding any options).

Lines of credit

A line of credit allows you to use equity from your principal place of residence or investment properties (both commercial property and residential are acceptable). It's an ongoing agreement between you and your bank that gives you access to a predetermined amount of credit whenever you need it. With a line of credit mortgage, the money you borrow is usually secured against your equity in that property. It functions in a similar way to a credit card: you have a pre-approved credit limit and can borrow as much of this as you want, paying interest on the outstanding balance.

If you're using another property as security against the line of credit, you present a lower risk to the lender and will generally pay a lower interest rate than on other forms of debt. However, because one of your properties is being used as equity for another, if your investments go down in value, you may lose both properties.

Note that a line of credit is not amortised – that is, your regular payments don't reduce or pay off the debt.

Split loans

A split loan has multiple accounts that attract different interest rates; you can allocate as much as you want to each account, as long as it's allowed by your lender. A split loan has two components: a portion that a fixed interest rate applies to and another portion to which a variable rate applies. This allows you to manage the risk of interest-rate fluctuations in times of economic uncertainty in the fixed component and, at the same time, take advantage if rates drop with the variable component.

Refinancing

Refinancing isn't a type of loan per se: it's the process of obtaining a new mortgage in an effort to reduce monthly payments, lower your interest rates, take cash for another purchase, or change lenders. By revaluing and refinancing, you may be able to free up equity to invest further.

Commercial bill facility

A commercial bill helps you raise the finance you need for investment purposes. A commercial bill is a promise made by a client to pay the bank a specified amount (the 'face value' of the bill) on a specified future date (the maturity date).

Commercial bills are used by sophisticated or seasoned investors, and can be an excellent solution when you need more than $100,000. Normal terms are from one to six months for variable rates and from one to five years for fixed rates. The interest rate, or 'floor' rate, is based on the bank bill swap rate (BBSW) and a margin, called the 'facility fee', of 1 to 3 per cent, which the lender adds. This margin can vary significantly among lenders, depending on factors that include the financial strength of the borrower, the underlying security and competitive pressures.

Vendor finance

One less publicised but quite common avenue for obtaining finance for a commercial property is vendor finance, also known as 'seller finance' or an 'instalment sale'. As commercial properties usually require at least a 30 per cent deposit, when you add on purchasing costs, the capital required for an investment can be quite high.

Trying to come up with this amount of funding can halt an investor's portfolio expansion.

With vendor finance, the vendor or seller makes money by on-selling their property to a buyer using a lease option or an instalment contract to provide all or part of the funds. In essence, the buyer borrows funds from the seller to buy the property. It's comparable to buying residential properties from developers that offer you the option to buy with little or no deposit.

When vendor financing is being used, the vendor needs to own the property they're selling outright (unencumbered), or at least have a debt level low enough to be able to pay it off from your LVR or their resources. The seller also needs to agree to the terms of seller financing and on the other side, the buyer will need to trust the new owner and their ability to pay them back.

The buyer makes principal and interest payments to the seller, usually monthly. The title will either be transferred straight away or once the final repayment is paid to the seller, depending on the vendor finance type.

There are three common forms of vendor finance:

1. **Terms finance/instalment sale.** With this method, the value of the property is repaid in instalments and the title remains with the vendor until either the final instalment is paid or the buyer refinances the loan with a bank and the title is transferred. The duration of the contract can be as long as required, but normally a purchaser pays it out as soon as they can refinance, which is usually within two to five years.

2. **Mortgage-backed finance.** With this type, the vendor loan is used as the deposit finance. The deposit is funded by the vendor using an external party. The vendor funds the difference between the price and the external finance and takes security for payment through a second mortgage over the property. The title will be transferred to the buyer right away.

3. **Lease option finance.** In this type, the property is leased to the purchaser, who makes additional payments towards the deposit on the purchase. This method works well if the buyer is an investor or business owner who'd like to operate out of the premises but does not have the required deposit. Much like mortgage-backed finance, the title is generally transferred right away.

Vendor finance usually has a fixed end date when a lump sum may be due, which is known as a 'balloon payment'. This can be paid in cash or by refinancing the property. It's essential that you don't make the balloon payment due date too soon to execute, otherwise you could face foreclosure or loss of the property if you don't have the funds available in time.

As you saw in Chapter 11, it's possible to buy a commercial property with 100 per cent of the costs financed and still be cash-flow positive. If you can negotiate vendor-finance terms for all or part of the purchase price, you'll be able to buy more properties without being limited by the banks and your capital.

As a buyer, you might consider vendor financing for the following reasons, as well:

- **Minimal savings.** If you're unable to provide the required deposit for the property but are able to service the loan, vendor finance will provide the time and flexibility to purchase the property

- **Short or poor credit history.** If you have a poor credit rating or a short credit history, it may be hard to qualify for a loan with a lender, and vendor finance may be a good option

- **Self-employment.** If you're the owner of a business that has been operating for fewer than two years, or you haven't demonstrated financial discipline or saving, banks may be reluctant to lend to you.

You can also sell your own properties using vendor finance. The typical purchaser would be either the occupier of a property, or an investor who is quite able to service a loan but is capital-poor. Both buyers may have the same problems – either not being able to raise the deposit or not being able to meet a lender's borrowing criteria. A seller may consider vendor financing if they:

- are more interested in getting the highest price for the property rather than getting cash at the time of sale

- have a sense of security and trusts in the property's long-term prospects – if the new buyer fails to repay as specified, they're willing to retake possession of the property

- don't need all the cash from the sale immediately and are happy to have a solid return

- can reduce their capital gains tax obligations by not cashing out all the property at once – vendor financing can allow them to spread the gains across multiple years and so reduce their tax

- are desperate for the sale and therefore more open to non-conservative offers

- are personally attached to the property and want to ensure it goes to the right owner long term.

However, vendor finance carries significant risks to the buyer that may outweigh its potential benefits, as follows:

- If the property depreciates in value over time, the bank may not lend you (the buyer) the money to refinance (market risk).

- The purchase price and subsequent repayments are normally higher than market value, which will make it harder for you to build equity and to qualify for a loan when you need to refinance.

- As your name may not be on the title, your ownership is at risk – for example, if the vendor goes bankrupt, others may make claims against the property.

- The laws regulating vendor finance are extremely cloudy, and so the buyer can often be at the mercy of the seller – sellers could, for example, be far more aggressive when dealing with even minor defaults than, say, a major bank.

The risks to the seller are relatively minimal, as they will usually own the property until the vendor finance is repaid. The seller only risks to losing the money provided to the buyer; and this is usually mitigated by having adequate security from them.

Vendor finance may seem like a good solution if you're a borrower who will have trouble raising a deposit or who'll fall outside lenders' criteria, but it's crucial to seek the advice of a solicitor to make sure your interests are protected before you enter into any agreement.

CHAPTER TWENTY-SIX

THE LOAN PROCESS

Brokers and lenders cannot give you a definitive pre-approval for a commercial property loan as they can with residential property, because commercial yields, conditions and risk can vary considerably. Also, finance is generally very property-specific for commercial loans – lenders will want to consider the property, its location, the tenant and the rental return, whereas with residential property this is less of an issue. While lender pre-approvals for commercial purchases are possible, they are generally looser than for residential properties.

So, once the contract of sale is signed, it's sent to the broker or lender so they can begin processing your loan. Finance approval is typically the most stressful part of the property purchase, and sometimes extensions of time are needed. Lenders often respond slowly, give poor valuations and require you to submit a large number of documents – mostly in hard copy. Valuations can also be unpredictable due to the difficulty in finding comparable properties. The larger your portfolio, the more complicated the lending and valuation procedure becomes.

If the contract is subject to finance or due diligence, you'll be trying to obtain finance at the same time. It's critical that your mortgage broker and lender have all the information they need from the start of the process, including proof of your personal information and financial history.

Your personal information

A formal proof of identification check may be required if you haven't borrowed from a particular lender before. This can usually be organised at your local post office and may require you to present your passport, driver's licence, birth certificate, and government identification cards such as Medicare.

You will also need to give details about the length of time you have been at your current address. Information about the number and ages of any dependants you have (children or otherwise) and your relationship status, as your partner may also be responsible for the loan.

Your financial situation

Lenders will look at your banking history – ideally, you'll have had stable and regular income and expenses for at least two years to maximise your chances. It's fairly obvious that you should try to avoid unpaid debts, bankruptcies and legal monetary matters that would affect your capacity to service a new loan.

You'll need to supply detailed information about your finances, which may include details of:

- your assets, including proof of your savings history, your bank accounts, current properties and any other investments such as shares
- your living expenses and outgoings
- your credit cards, store and charge cards, including statements
- any history of defaults or arrears

- proof of employment
- proof of income and government payments
- bank statements showing income up to six months back
- group certificates, tax returns, tax assessment notices and balance sheets for the most recent financial year.

If you're struggling to obtain finance, as a last resort you can request an extension of the finance period under contract. Many agents and sellers understand the harsh lending environment and will usually agree when given a valid reason.

Note that it's usually more difficult to obtain finance for a vacant property, because you need to prove that you can get a certain rent for the space. Lenders really focus on the cash flow a commercial property might produce.

They look well on a strong lease and, in particular, on how long is left on the lease. So, if the tenant has less than one year left, it's worth asking if they would exercise their renewal option now as the lenders will look favourably on this. In many cases you'll need to give the tenant an incentive to take up the option, such as halting rental increases for the term or slightly reducing the rent.

If you have other properties and are using equity from them as the deposit, you need to assess which properties it would be best to leverage and compare the interest-rate differences. Because commercial property loans typically have a higher interest rate, leveraging a principal place of residence or a residential property can save you quite a lot in interest repayments. The lender will also value the property nominated as security, unless a line of credit is used.

The five Cs of credit

It's also a good idea to consider the 'five Cs of credit': character, capacity, capital, collateral and conditions. Lenders use this analysis to determine the risk associated with a loan.

Character

Lenders want to know if you, the borrower, and any guarantors are honest and have integrity. Character in this context amounts to your willingness to pay back the mortgage. The lender needs to be confident you have the background, education and stability of employment to do this, and will also verify whether you have a criminal record. Banks will sometimes give better rates or higher LVRs to people in certain professions – usually white-collar or government jobs that are stable with a lower risk of unemployment.

A lender will examine the personal credit of all borrowers and guarantors involved and will want to ensure that your past financial information is sound and regular. If you have any delinquencies, be prepared to explain them.

Capacity

Capacity means serviceability, or your ability to repay a loan. Lenders base their assessment of your capacity on a number of factors, including your income, the loan amount, your age, and your other commitments and expenses. The bank uses these factors to calculate a debt service ratio (DSR), which is the percentage of your monthly income expected to be spent on debts. The bank will want the DSR to be below a specific number, which will vary among lenders.

When considering your income, the lender will take into account things such as overtime, commissions and company cars. Depending on your profession and how frequent your overtime is, though, the bank may take only a portion of it into its calculations.

There are restrictions about counting income from a second job: you'll need to have been receiving this income for a certain period before it can be included, and each lender has its own criteria to determine how much of this income will be counted. Your serviceability and how much you can borrow will therefore depend heavily on your choice of lender.

Lenders will generally consider only a portion of the rental income you receive from a commercial property, and will take account of the strength of the lease, the property's location and vacancy rates. This allows a buffer for any vacancy periods you may experience and is known by lenders as 'shading the property'.

Lenders will also calculate repayments by adding a margin interest-rate percentage (about 2.5 per cent or more) to the variable rate. This 'assessment rate' is used to predict whether you'd be able to meet repayments if there were an interest-rate rise.

Your regular and irregular outgoings will be considered as well, of course. These include regular expenses, credit-card debts (and their limits), car loans, student loans, and the number of children or dependants living in your home. These can all negatively affect your loan serviceability and make it much harder to obtain finance. To increase your chances, it's essential to minimise the limits on all credit cards and always pay any personal and car loans on time.

Capital

Capital represents the wealth of the borrower(s) and any assets or valuables that make up their total net worth. In short, it's the value of your assets minus your liabilities. The lender considers your savings, investments such as real estate and shares, the value of your car and other assets, minus any personal loans and credit card and other debts. Lenders would like to see that you have a buffer that would allow you to keep paying your loan if you had a financial setback such as losing your job. By looking at your capital, lenders assess your ability and willingness to save and accumulate assets and then compare this with your age.

Collateral

Collateral is an important consideration, but its significance varies with the type of loan. Generally speaking, collateral is represented by the properties used to secure the loan. If you are cross-collateralising (using another property as security to obtain the loan) the properties and are unable to make the agreed repayments, the bank has the right to seize your property to repay the debt. However, before they do this, they usually explore all other avenues, including reducing or freezing the repayments for a period. If the lender does end up selling your property, you retain any capital gains from the sale.

If you can't provide collateral or security in the form of property, some lenders offer guarantor loans, which use a third party's collateral as a backup.

Conditions

'Conditions' refers to the financial conditions at the time you submit your application – specifically your interest rate, principal amount and general market conditions. It encompasses any outside circumstances that may affect your financial situation and ability to make loan repayments.

Lenders may evaluate the overall business climate, both within your industry and in associated industries, and the economic conditions that could affect your borrowing, including the Reserve Bank's cash rate and any policy changes that affect borrowers' ability to borrow money. These factors can affect the lender's allowable LVR on the property.

Valuations

Valuations for commercial properties are not the same as those for a residential property, which usually involve only a desktop valuation performed free of charge. Most lenders will offer a free valuation on a residential property every 12 months. Commercial valuations are very detailed and usually cost between $800 and $3,000 for a standard property.

Once a property has become 'conditional', lenders will usually give you the names of three valuation companies that are on their panel. It's best to call each valuer to see how knowledgeable they are and to find out their costs, which can vary widely. It's also worth speaking with agents about recent sales, which may not show up immediately on databases or can take months to be uploaded. If these work in your favour, it's a good idea to let the valuer know about them. If you can provide useful information to them, you may get a better result.

On existing properties in your portfolio, it's worth speaking with the valuer before paying for a valuation. Ask what cap rate they are applying to similar properties, as this will give you a good indication of the valuation you'll obtain and whether it's worthwhile spending money on another valuation and refinancing to extract the equity.

The valuer will inspect the property before writing a report. Valuation reports go into quite a lot of detail, similar to the due diligence you should have performed yourself. They'll include:

- a synopsis of the property
- critical assumptions made
- the investment profile
- a risk profile or SWOT (strengths, weaknesses, opportunities, threats) analysis
- the title details
- town planning information
- a site description
- information regarding improvements
- photos
- a financial analysis
- details of other income
- outgoings

- rental evidence
- rental reconciliation
- sales evidence
- sales reconciliation
- a valuation rationale (whether a capitalisation approach or direct comparison approach was used)
- additional reporting.

Note that when you're buying a commercial property at auction, the lenders will generally use the purchase price as the property's value, because the price was established through fair market competition.

Under-market valuations are common, because valuers take a very cautious approach. If the valuation does not come back as you expected, you can renegotiate the purchase price, contest the valuation, look for another valuer, or walk away from the deal. If you do renegotiate the property price because of a poor valuation, you need to analyse carefully why the banks valued it lower than you expected. You can also pay the difference to get the deal done if you think it's a good property.

If more time is needed, you can ask for an extension of finance – but if the extension is denied, you then need to terminate the contract to avoid penalties. Usually, the seller will give you a few days' extension, sometimes a couple of weeks if they really want the sale to go ahead as soon as possible. They can even give you a conditional extension that enables them to advertise or go under contract with another buyer if you don't respond in time.

Importantly, though: don't be afraid to walk away if you can potentially not complete the sale or it's just not working. As I've said before, the costs you've spent on the deal up to this point are insignificant compared with having a property that doesn't suit your needs.

If everything does check out and the valuation is acceptable, you can satisfy the contract's financing condition. Only after due diligence and building and pest inspections are complete is it recommended to go unconditional on the contract, however.

Before settlement day, your conveyancer will outline the funds available for settlement to occur and will work with the lender to ensure a smooth transfer of registrations. The lender will attend (either physically or online through PEXA) to the registration of the transfer, the release of the mortgage (if any) and registration of the loan at the Land Registry Services. The lender usually holds the property's title until the loan is paid off.

CHAPTER TWENTY-SEVEN

BUYING STRUCTURES AND SYNDICATES

Deciding the optimal ownership structure for your property investment can be confusing. It's vital to get it right, though, as it can save you thousands of dollars in tax and can also protect your personal assets in the event of bankruptcy. There is no one-size-fits-all solution, as everyone's situation is different, so obtain advice from a property tax expert (an accountant) about the best structure to use before you make an offer to buy a property.

The popular tax structures available to invest in property are:

- individual ownership in your name
- joint ownership with a partner or spouse
- a joint venture
- a family discretionary trust
- a unit trust
- a self-managed superannuation fund (SMSF)
- a company.

A property syndicate is a further option which can be beneficial in some situations.

Individual ownership

Investing in your own name is the simplest and most common method; it has no set-up cost and minimal compliance is required. One of the benefits of individual ownership is that you can negatively gear the property if there are any losses; however, as commercial property is usually positively geared, this may not be particularly beneficial.

On the down side, you could lose the property if you become bankrupt, even if your debts don't relate to the property.

Individual ownership is suitable for inexperienced property investors and for those who aren't concerned about the risk of bankruptcy.

Joint ownership with a partner or spouse

Joint ownership has similar implications to holding the property as an individual, but you'll need to consider the percentage of holding between the partners and whether you choose to be joint tenants or tenants in common.

Joint tenants

Joint tenants hold the property equally between them; the income or losses from the property are also split equally and added to the two partners' individual income-tax returns. If a joint tenant dies, the property automatically passes to the surviving joint tenant.

Tenants in common

A tenants-in-common arrangement means you decide the share each partner owns. As commercial properties are generally positively geared, so it can be advantageous to allocate a larger share to the spouse with the lower income. If the property is negatively geared, you would give the bigger share to the partner with the higher income to maximise the tax-deduction benefit.

If you're considering this structure, make sure you take into account your personal circumstances and also consider the impact of any future capital gains from a sale. If a party dies, the part ownership of the party who died passes as per their will.

A joint venture

A joint venture involves two or more individuals buying the property – they may be friends, family members or business partners. With this structure, in effect, you're entering a long-term relationship with the other person, and this needs to be clearly understood between the parties. It's important, therefore, to put all the terms of agreement in writing to avoid any possible legal difficulties later. Having an exit strategy is also vital, as individuals' circumstances can change dramatically over time, both financially and personally.

If possible, it's preferable to set up separate loans for each joint buyer. This means that if your partner struggles to make payments or defaults on the loan, it won't affect your borrowing capacity or credit history. Even if the joint venture runs smoothly, individual loans will be beneficial, because if, in the future, you want to borrow to invest in something separately, only your portion of the first loan will count against your ability to service a second loan. Without separate loans, the entire debt will count, even though someone else is paying half of it.

When you're buying as part of a group, it's essential that there's a consensus about how the property will be treated over time and the exit strategy. All members of the group need to have the same goals – whether to, for instance:

- sell the property in a short time, or hold it long term

- maximise the loan to value ratio in order to hold less capital in the deal, or maintain a modest LVR to maximise cash flow

- refinance the property at the earliest opportunity, or pay down the loan over time

- add value to the property by injecting capital, or spend less to have a higher short-term cash flow.

Some members may have a stable job and lifestyle, others may need to extract cash or sell for personal reasons. Others may not be able to get finance alone, and this may affect their goals for the investment. It's important that each member of the venture spells out their goals, and it's advisable for a contract to then be drawn up for the group to ensure everyone is protected legally.

A family discretionary trust

Holding a property in a family discretionary trust can be beneficial, as you don't need to specify the share of each spouse and family member, but have the flexibility to distribute income in the most tax-effective manner from year to year. A trust also protect assets (especially when you have a company as a trustee), and allows you to carry out estate and succession planning. Trusts are eligible for a 50 per cent discount on capital gains tax, as well.

The negative aspects of family discretionary trusts are that they cost quite a lot to set up, have a higher compliance cost for tax returns, and you can't distribute losses – which means they aren't suitable for holding negatively geared properties.

A unit trust

This differs from other trust structures in that the trustee divides the trust's property into fixed and quantifiable parts, called units. Beneficiaries subscribe to these units in a way similar to shareholders subscribing to shares in a company. Unit trusts provide the investors – 'unit holders' – with certainty, as the money or property from the trust is distributed to the beneficiaries in fixed proportions according to the number of units they hold. For this reason, unit trusts are more appropriate than discretionary trusts when third parties who are not family members are investing together.

The other benefits of a unit trust include asset protection (especially when you have a company as a trustee), estate and succession planning, and being eligible for a 50 per cent discount on capital gains tax.

A self-managed super fund

Self-managed superannuation funds (SMSF) are used when an individual wants to take full control of their superannuation assets, and many opt to buy commercial properties due to the high cash returns. Setting up an SMSF is costly, however, and takes a great deal of preparation, and managing it requires ongoing attention to ensure the many regulations are met.

Some of the tax benefits are as follows:

- Once the individual or individuals retire, they pay no capital gains tax.

- Loan repayments can in effect become tax-deductible (provided members salary sacrifice).

- Income (after expenses and any capital gains on the disposal of property) is taxed at a maximum rate of 15 per cent, compared with the up to 46.5 per cent that a regular investor could be paying.

- Employer superannuation contributions can be used to help repay any loan associated with the property, and can be protected against general debt recovery and bankruptcy proceedings.

One point to note is that any tenants you have in an SMSF property must be third party and not related to you.

A company

A company is a legal entity in its own right; when you borrow in the name of a company, it will own the investment property. The company will be the borrower and all directors of the company will be required to guarantee the loan.

Some of the benefits of buying under a company structure are a lower tax rate, the ability to plan tax through dividends, the fact that the tax paid by the company can be franked (i.e. passed on as credit to shareholders with dividends), and that it provides a much higher level of protection for your assets outside the company.

However, financing is usually harder for companies to obtain, due to banking restrictions, and you risk losing the property if your company is sued.

Some other drawbacks are that the set-up and maintenance costs of a company structure are quite high, and companies aren't eligible for the 50 per cent discount on capital gains that's available to trusts or individuals. A company cannot distribute losses, either, so this isn't a suitable structure if your property is negatively geared. Another issue is that although, as a director of the company, you won't be personally liable for its debts, you will be legally obligated for responsibilities such as ensuring solvent trading (in other words, for ensuring the company doesn't trade while insolvent).

Syndicates

Property syndicates pool funds from many investors to acquire a commercial property for the financial benefit of all. They offer qualifying 'sophisticated investors' the opportunity to part-own high-quality, expensive commercial real estate that would ordinarily be beyond their reach. Syndicates also enable the investor to be more passive – less involved with the tenancies and management of the property.

The term 'sophisticated' investor is defined in the *Corporations Act* and denotes a professional investor, so this isn't an ownership structure that's available to beginning investors or those on a lower income. To qualify as a sophisticated investor, you'll need a signed confirmation (Sophisticated Investor Certificate) from your accountant that you own assets of more than $2.5 million or earned more than $250,000 in each of the previous two financial years. If you invest $500,000 or more in a syndicated offering, however, you're not required to provide a Sophisticated Investor Certificate.

A syndicate is legally structured as a unit trust, with investors applying for ordinary units in the trust. In many respects, a unit trust is similar to a company; as mentioned earlier, units have most of the same characteristics as company shares. However, syndicates are usually established for a finite period – about five years – after which it is intended (but not mandated) that the asset be sold. Syndicates will guarantee ordinary unit-holders the right to cash out their investment after five years, whether or not the property is sold at that time. The trustee has the right to sell the property and wind up the trust before five years if it considers that to be in the best interests of unit holders.

The syndicate trust's formation and management are delegated to an associated company: it handles finding the property or properties and negotiating the purchase; performing due diligence on the properties; organise financing arrangements; maintaining all financial records; dealing with real estate agents, property managers, tenants, maintenance contractors; and the day-to-day running of affairs.

Note that the operators of the syndicate are required to hold an Australian Financial Services Licence (AFSL) which imposes comprehensive and strenuous obligations on the licensee. The principals of the licensee must possess extensive relevant experience and the appropriate degree of expertise. Licenses are tightly regulated and the company will be audited annually, with the auditors certifying that the company is complying with all of its legal and statutory obligations. The affairs and finances of each unit trust the licensee manages are also audited individually every year.

As with other trusts, an agreement governs the relationship between all parties and stipulates key terms and conditions. A regularly used term in the agreement for syndicates is the 'objective', which identifies the reasons for creating the property syndicate. The goals are typically shared across the group.

In summary, for the right investor, a syndicate is a way to invest in many properties without owning them completely, and to purchase expensive large-scale commercial real estate properties that would otherwise be out of reach. Some syndicates are organised privately between investors, but there are companies that will organise the syndicate. The benefits include:

- **Less capital required.** Individual investors are able to buy higher-valued properties with less capital as there are multiple investors.

- **Diversification.** Having a smaller outlay by being part of a syndicate allows you to spread the risk over multiple properties.

- **Stable returns.** By diversifying your assets, you're able regulate your returns and have less volatility.

- **Time saving.** Investing in a syndicate requires less effort than finding and securing a property yourself, and you'll spend less time on management and administrative matters.

The risks of investing in a syndicate include:

- **Less control.** Since there will be multiple investors, you have less say in decisions.

- **Other vested interests and transparency.** The financial interests, goals and wishes of the other investors need to be taken into account. They can sometimes have hidden their intentions, however, and it's important to acknowledge that other investors' goals and personal and financial situations may change.

- **Management issues.** Investing in a syndicate leaves control in the hands of a management team, and this requires a level of trust. Seeking regular updates from the team will help to avoid potential issues, however.

PART VII
POST-PURCHASE

Finding, vetting and buying the right commercial property is vital to making a profitable investment, as you've seen in the book thus far. The other piece of the puzzle, of course, is what you do post-purchase. Once the property is yours, it's important to manage it well, and to make any upgrades, additions or changes which could add value to the property. This part of the book is devoted to the important topics of good property management and value-adding, and the last chapter will explore the strategies and approaches that will help you survive downturns.

CHAPTER TWENTY-EIGHT

PROPERTY MANAGEMENT

Managing a tenanted commercial property sometimes appears to be easy and to require little time. Since the tenant is often responsible for all outgoings, it might seem the only job is making sure the rent is paid on time! But there's quite a lot more to it than that, which is why many investors engage a professional property manager. You need to keep track of:

- **The tenants** – their rent payments, outgoing payments, rental increases, lease renewals and any breaches of lease

- **Record keeping** – including rent receipts, outgoing receipts, rates notices, regulation notices such as fire checks, council permits and updates to the *Retail Leases Act*

- **Repairs and maintenance** – organising repairs, liaising with the tenant, engaging local maintenance contractors, understanding maintenance costs and quotes and becoming familiar with the building

- **Rent** – know the current market and the *Retail Leases Act*, manage rent reviews and lease options, keep track of rental arrears, do bank reconciliations

- **Tenancy disputes** – for which you'll need dispute-resolution skills, a high level of communication skills and negotiation ability

- **Finding new tenants** – marketing and advertising for new tenants, and reviewing new tenants.

Having a strong, detailed lease that stipulates what's required of the tenant will assist in covering all the above issues, but they still need to be managed day to day.

Self-management vs using a property manager

As you can see, there's quite a lot of management involved, so you need to assess how much time you have, and also whether you can give enough attention to the detail and have the right personality to resolve disputes. It's also critical to have the correct software and methods to manage the property.

The main reason most people manage their properties themselves is to save money and increase their cash flow, or because they don't want to trust someone else with their investment. However, poor property management can cost a huge amount of time, money and stress. If you're time-poor and your effort is better directed elsewhere, a property manager may be the better answer.

On the other hand, if you have the time and the necessary personality traits, you may manage the property better than a property manager would, because for you it's a personal investment.

If you are managing the property yourself, you need to be available 24/7, as issues – whether minor or otherwise – can arise at any time. You'll also need to make time to assess tenant applications and conduct tenant interviews.

It's wise not to become too friendly with the tenant, because the relationship can be difficult if things go wrong with the tenancy. Having a property manager can be an advantage here, as it can create a level of separation between the tenant and owner.

Selecting a property manager

The right property manager can be the difference between a property that is tenanted long term and a vacant one. Your relationship with the manager is a partnership. You're looking for a long-term relationship, as the manager will be instrumental in ensuring that your property produces a positive result. You need a good rapport and communication so that the manager understands your objectives and finds the right tenants for your space.

Look for a property manager who sees his or her job as about relationship building, not just completing transactions. Their focus should be on increasing the value of your asset while maintaining and increasing cash flow each year.

Finding a manager who has experience in your property's type, size and location will give you a better outcome. Local knowledge is extremely important, and obviously you need them to be close by to handle tenant issues. You also want your manager to have a good reputation in the community.

The manager also, of course, needs to be up to date with modern, digital-based electronic resources and must digitise all hard copy media such as bills, maintenance invoices and cheques received.

One point to be aware of is that the selling agent for a property you've purchased may push to manage it after the sale. However, just because they sold the property doesn't necessarily mean they're the best person to manage it. One of the best ways to find a good manager is by referral from another commercial property investor – there are now many online commercial-investor groups on social media, so asking for referrals has become relatively easy.

If possible, it's always best to visit a potential property manager at their office so you can get a feel for their staff and their organisational skills. If everything's untidy and there are mountains of files on every surface, it can be a sign that they're overwhelmed.

Here are some questions you should ask them:

- How long has the company been in business?

- How long has your dedicated property manager been at the business and what's their previous management experience?

- How many residential and commercial properties does the business manage?

- How many residential and commercial properties does your dedicated property manager manage?

- Does your dedicated property manager have a personal assistant?

- Is there a separate team for residential and commercial property?

- How often are routine inspections carried out?

- Could you give me some examples of other properties you manage in the area?

- What's the typical time to re-let a property similar to mine? Could you give some examples?

- How do you run your marketing campaigns?

- What's the procedure for tenant reviews?

- What's the procedure for collecting arrears?

You want to know whether they have well thought-through process, and to see how they compare with other companies. A good property manager will have a solution to a problem before they inform you of it, and when there's a vacancy, a good property manager will be proactive in advertising it and include you in all steps of the process. Importantly, they should communicate well with you – if your potential property manager is slow to respond to your calls or emails, you may want to consider someone else.

Engaging a property manager

Once you have appointed a property manager, they will send you the paperwork needed to authorise them to carry out management activities. Many property managers will let you sign the documents electronically, usually through www.docusign.com.au.

After this, depending on whether you previously managed the property yourself or you're moving from another management service, you'll need to obtain and provide or just provide the following to your new manager:

- the lease agreements

- copies of current and outstanding invoices

- the dates on which each tenant pays rent

- how much any bonds are for and where they're held

- whether outgoings are paid on demand or allocated monthly, and the current amount

- the settlement statement, if you've just purchased.

Note that in contrast with residential properties, where the bond is in the property manager's trust account, bonds for commercial properties can be held by the owner's choosing, even in their own personal bank account. Many investors elect to have them held in their own account as it enables control and the funds can be invested.

The manager will then contact each of your tenants about future procedures. Ideally, at this point, your work is largely finished and you'll have a 'set and forget' property.

Property manager costs

A typical commercial property will take a couple hours a month on average from the manager for invoicing and general management.

Most property-management charges are based on a percentage of the gross rent, calculated on a tiered approach. Managing a lower renting property requires the same amount of work as a higher renting property, so managers charge a higher percentage to earn the same money.

The fees can vary between 3.5 per cent and 7 per cent of the gross, and are very much negotiable. However, in general, if you have a tenant paying $300,000 a year, the fee will be closer to 2 per cent, whereas if you have a tenant paying only $30,000 a year, the owner will most likely be paying closer to 7 per cent. Most property managers will expect to be paid $1,500 to $5,000 a year.

Their fees are tax-deductible to the owner, so overall there is not much financial gain taking on the management responsibilities yourself. In some cases, it's drafted into the lease agreement that the tenant is responsible for paying the management fee as an outgoing.

Typical fee structure

As mentioned, all fees can be negotiated. For instance, you could handle a rent review yourself and perhaps save yourself 10 per cent of the annual income fee. It's best to negotiate any such reductions before you engage the manager, and to record the details on the agency agreement. Beware of hidden fees – some managers will charge you for each extra service.

Following is a typical fee structure showing possible fees during the ownership.

Task	Fee (+ GST)	Timing
General management, including: • invoicing and collection of rent (and outgoings) • disbursements to clients • payment of accounts • issuing of notice to remedy a breach	5.5% of annual income	Payable upon each collection under the lease, taken when funds are disbursed
Lease renewal or negotiating new terms	10% of annual income	Payable either upon the signing of the agreement, lease or extension, or the start of a new or extended term, whichever is earlier. (Each party pays its own solicitors' fees.)
Option extension (deed or form 13 via solicitors)	10 to 50% of monthly income	
Rent review, fixed rent review, fixed/CPI rent review	$0.00 to $500.00	For most managers, this is payable within 7 days of completion of the review. The fee will usually be added to the next disbursement
Issuing notices to remedy a breach in particular circumstances to lease	$0.00 to $350.00	This will usually be included in the general management fee, but can be charged separately

Task	Fee (+ GST)	Timing
Issuing notices to terminate, serving these, and lock out, and preparation, liaising and attending any tribunal on enforcement matters	$150 an hour	Payable within 7 days of invoice
All out of pocket expenses	As incurred	When paid

Selecting and managing a tenant

As with choosing a property or a property manager, when you're selecting a tenant, it's essential to perform due diligence before signing a lease. The following checklist details things to look for when vetting tenants.

Tenant checklist

☐ Get references from previous landlords if possible.

☐ How long have they been in business?

☐ What was their previous location and why did they move?

☐ If they're a startup, ask about their business plan.

☐ Request a rental ledger or at least three months of bank statements.

☐ Do they appear to be capable operators, with a long-term business?

☐ Check the owners' identity.

☐ Run a credit check on the owners and the business.

☐ What is the owners' general presentation like?

☐ Request evidence of their assets.

☐ Do they have experience in the business they're proposing to operate as your tenant?

Note that new businesses are a risky proposition and failure rates are high. You need to work out whether the prospective tenant will be good for you long term, or whether you'd be better off keeping the property vacant until you find a better tenant. The answer will depend partly on supply and demand in your location.

Your relationship with the tenant is very important. Some properties, especially big retail ones, will have onsite managers you need to deal with as well, and this relationship is equally crucial. A common issue with tenants is their lack of understanding of the lease requirements in regards to their responsibilities, so try to ensure you or the property manager explain these clearly at the outset, before the lease is signed. Also, don't hesitate to contact your solicitor with any questions about your tenant and the lease.

Tenants are usually responsible for property maintenance, but this will depend on the lease. Be careful if you're buying a property with an expensive fit-out such as refrigeration or a commercial kitchen, as even if you're not responsible for these during the lease, if you have ultimate ownership of them, when the tenant leaves you could be up for maintenance while the property is vacant.

You want the property to be well maintained, but in the most cost-effective way so the tenant's expenses are minimised. Having a cost-saving, savvy property manager will assist with this. This will encourage them to stay on and help to ensure that their business remains profitable too.

Outgoings such as rates and electricity need to be paid and charged on to the tenant if these are their responsibility, but note that they will still need your attention. The property manager will usually need to get involved, for example, if the electricity, heating or water is not working correctly.

It's important to keep electronic records of everything, including dates, times and requests. And make sure all your correspondence remains very professional, as if things go wrong you might end up in a tribunal or court situation.

Tenant mix

For multi-tenancy properties, the tenant mix and tenant compatibility can be important in the success or failure of a business. As commercial leases are comparatively long, it can be difficult to correct mistakes in a timely manner. You will try to get the mix right as soon as possible, so a review at the end of each lease is essential. Commercial tenants will often place a high value on a property's image and reputation, and they'll want to be near businesses that complement their own or increase the foot traffic or exposure to their business. One tenant's business can thus contribute to the success of the others.

So, when you're choosing a new tenant, it's best to analyse what kinds of businesses will fit well with the others. Communicate with your existing tenants to ensure that there are no clashes or competing businesses. Complementary services can work well together, but on the other hand, a wide variety of tenants can bring more foot traffic to the property.

Rental increases

We went into detail about rental increases in Chapter 7, but let's quickly return to the topic as it relates to dealing with tenants.

Obviously, you as a landlord will want to maximise a property's rental return and yield – however, this doesn't always mean getting the highest market rent or imposing rental increases. There's a balance to be struck between keeping tight vacancies and obtaining the top market rent.

New or inexperienced commercial investors are more likely to be guilty of raising rents too soon or too quickly – generally, steady increases are best unless there is huge demand for the property and you're being paid below market value.

Tenants, on their part, will weigh up what they're paying against what they're receiving, so it's essential to provide them with good value. The benefits of this over the long term will outweigh the short-term gains from high rents. It costs a lot more to secure a new tenant than to retain an existing one, and along with these upfront costs, you're incurring the risk of taking on a new business. Your highest priority should therefore be retaining occupancy to give you the best long-term return.

Rents should be increased with care, as this can put a lot of personal, emotional and business strain on the tenant, and they could feel the need to investigate other options. They'll respond better to rental increases when they can see they're receiving more value, perhaps because you're providing better facilities.

Note that sometimes, fixed rental increases can put rents above market value. If this happens, it can be worth lowering the rent to keep the tenant. However, reducing the rent, for whatever reason, does lower the value of the property. So, when faced with a choice between finding a new tenant or reviewing the rent for your existing tenant, it's better to offer one or more months of free rent rather than a rent reduction.

CHAPTER TWENTY-NINE

VALUE-ADDING

Due to their variety, commercial properties offer many more possibilities than residential property when it comes to adding value. If you can see opportunities to add value to a property when you're viewing it with the selling agent, keep that information to yourself! It could discourage the seller from giving you good deal.

Here are some ways you may be able to add value:

- **Changing the property's use.** A property can be repurposed, in part or overall. This could involve converting an unused or common area space into lettable space, or upgrading a storage area to office or industrial space.

- **Raising or lowering rents.** It's wise to constantly review market rents, but raising them needs to be done on a case-by-case basis, as mentioned in the previous chapter. Keeping a tenant or maintaining low vacancy levels is paramount.

- **Improving the property's quality and image.** This will command higher rents and increase the property's yield and value. Renovations such as refurbishing, painting and landscaping can make a dramatic difference. Sometimes, these will even be initiated by the tenant at no cost to the owner.

- **Creating new sources of revenue.** Some examples are installing automated teller machines (ATMs), solar power charge-back incentives, vending machines, renting out parking or storage space, taking on off-peak rentals, allowing advertising space, installing mobile phone towers and repeaters, and offering a serviced office.

- **Adding or upgrading the property marketing.** Additional marketing can boost rents and lower vacancies. This can be as simple as having better street signage, a website or targeted advertising. This will create demand for your location and provide a higher rental rate.

- **Removing underperforming tenants.** This is particularly applicable in retail centres, where one underperforming tenant can reduce foot traffic, create competition for another tenant, or give rise to a poor culture in the centre.

- **Improving the property management.** Good property management is essential, as discussed in Chapter 28.

- **Development.** As with residential properties, it's possible to develop commercial properties. This could involve subdivision, building new buildings, or adding an extra storey to increase the value and/or cash flow.

EXAMPLE: Adding telecommunications base stations

Here's a simple example of a creative addition in value to a commercial property – the corner fish and chip shop shown in the photo below. This property has three income streams: the takeaway restaurant, a residential apartment on top of the restaurant, and the letting of the roof space for telecommunication devices. A small rent concession would be provided to both tenants because of the eyesore on the roof, but the addition of these devices would hugely increase your cash flow. Council permission must be sought for value-add items such as this, of course.

If you're looking to expand your portfolio quickly, it's important not to set and forget – you need to always be on the lookout for ways to improve your properties' value. Even increasing the rent will probably raise the value of your property.

Check the zoning and planning laws every two years: ask a local town planner to see if there has been any change to the zoning, to floor space ratio rules, or anything else that may affect the property. As mentioned previously, it's best to use an independent town planner, as they're generally more experienced and are motivated to help in the hope of receiving future work from you.

It's also worth speaking with your tenant every six months about what could be done to improve the property. Quite often, a tenant may wish to improve the shopfront's presentation but doesn't have the money to do it – if you pay for the work, and then charge extra rent to recoup the cost, you not only have a happy tenant, but the higher rent will also have increased the value of the property.

CHAPTER THIRTY

SURVIVING A DOWNTURN

You may experience a downturn in your investments for many reasons – it could be the economy, the demand for your type of commercial premises, an act of God or because your tenant's business is struggling. In these circumstances, the ability and value of your property manager, if you're using one, will really shine.

You can mitigate the risk of downturns in general by buying a versatile commercial property that is flexible and could have multiple uses – for instance, a retail space that could be turned into office space. This could reduce the length of vacancy if the tenant unexpectedly gave up the tenancy.

Let's look now at ways to survive downturns that occur for some of the specific reasons mentioned above.

A decline in the industry or the tenant's business

If your tenant's business is struggling, you have a number of options. You could, for example, assist them with costs of renovations, installing air conditioning or by offering one or more months' free rent. The tenant's business is in effect your business, so knowing when to give a concession and show compassion is important.

However, a rental reduction or free rent won't necessarily solve the tenant's problem. The downward momentum when a business starts to struggle is usually hard to stop.

So, you need to know when your tenant's financial situation is irrecoverable and when to cut the assistance. Try not to get emotionally involved. Most tenants see their landlord as a wealthy individual with lots of spare cash, so they might be inclined to try to take advantage of your generosity. On the other side, tenants will sometime blame their business's difficulties on the quality of the property.

Staying calm and sticking to the terms of the lease as much as possible is generally good advice. Either party can be held accountable if the terms are not adhered to, including not paying the rent or the outgoings required. If a tenant is in breach of the lease, you or your property manager need to act quickly to get on top of any issues and mitigate losses.

It's imperative, of course, to have a strong and detailed lease, as this can help mitigate any issues with the tenant and save you money in the long run.

When the issue is first noticed, contact the tenant immediately to see if it can be rectified. If the tenant is late on rent, find out when they can pay it; it may be appropriate to accept a partial payment and give a deadline for the rest. You then need to check that it is paid on the agreed date. If not, ask the tenant to provide an electronic copy of the receipt, in case the payment has been made but hasn't yet cleared in your account.

If payment isn't made, it's time to contact your solicitor and to tell the tenant that they're in breach of the lease. A breach of lease notice is then served on the tenant, outlining the issue to be addressed and by what time it needs to be done. If the breach isn't remedied, you may need to take further action, such as locking the tenant out of the property.

If it appears the tenant won't be able to rectify the breach, start advertising for a new tenant as soon as possible. You can also take legal action against the tenant to recover any losses incurred, such as lost rent (until the property is re-let), outgoings that the tenant should have paid, and advertising costs to find a new tenant. Usually, the maximum loss you can recoup is the rent that would have been payable until the end of the lease option. In the worst case, you should have the bond or bank guarantee to fall back on during this time.

During this process, both parties should seek legal action to help mitigate damages and risk.

To reiterate, though, it's best to try to work with the tenant through these issues. Sometimes their business is seasonal, which may produce unexpected costs that put them in a negative position. If the tenant can recover, keeping them is much better than eviction and legal action.

Acts of God

Throughout the English-speaking legal world, natural disasters such as earthquakes and tsunamis are referred to as 'acts of God' (also called 'force majeure events'). These are circumstances outside anyone's control that could not be foreseen or guarded against. Acts of God may provide a defence or an exception to liability, for example, in a situation that would otherwise be a breach of contract or a tort (a legal wrong which one person or entity commits against another person or entity, and for which the usual remedy is an award of damages).

Some events commonly classed as acts of God in Australia include floods, cyclones, bushfires and droughts. Recently, after COVID-19, legislation has been changed to say that the pandemic is considered an act of God, so insurance policies must be checked closely. It's essential to check whether building and landlord insurance will cover these possibilities, depending on the risk in the property's region. This needs to be assessed in the due diligence period before buying a property. You can also consider having a surveyor risk-assess your property and improve its resilience to such an event; for example, by undertaking bushfire-mitigation works on the land surrounding the property.

If your insurance doesn't cover these events, it's important to work with your tenant to ensure an optimal outcome for all. The most common solution in such a situation is for a period of free rent to be provided while the business is unable to operate, with this rent to be paid back later over time.

Global economic crises

As discussed in Chapter 12, the economy has quite an impact on property prices and business success, and so global economic crises will affect your commercial property. Depending on your tenant's industry, it may increase or decrease their business.

One of Australia's largest recent recessions occurred in 1990–91 – unemployment rose by about 5 per cent, the Australian share market dropped about 40 per cent, and the worst fall in any capital city was a maximum 2.3 per cent in capital value. Three of the capital cities actually grew during this time, to a maximum of 6.8 per cent, which demonstrates the stability of the properties.

Pandemics

At the time of writing, the COVID-19 pandemic has forced many businesses to shut, at least temporarily, or to operate online only. The pandemic will no doubt change the face of many sorts of commercial investment and also change the demand for certain property classes – an increase in industrial types and a shift from classic retail properties is likely, as more and more retailers go online.

Again, it's important to work with your tenants during these times and examine any claims they make about profit reduction, to see if a rent reduction would be fair. Consider the following steps:

1. **Refer to government incentives.** Some tenancies will not be affected by COVID-19 but may still ask the owner for a discount on their rent. In this case, suggest that the tenant explore the government grants available to small businesses under the stimulus measures announced. This is the first thing to do.

2. **Consider rent deferrals.** Some tenants may ask for their rent to be waived for the period they're unable to trade normally. However, it may be better to discount the rent to zero for a period (say, three months) and offer the option to sign a longer lease – at least 3 to 12 months more. This will strengthen your lease, improve your long-term income security and increase the value of your property once the pandemic is past. More importantly, your tenant will remain in business!

3. **Consider rent relief.** Rent relief or a discount may turn out to be the best option, in the end, as you want your tenant to be still in business in 12 months' time. One strategy is to discount the rent by, say, 50 per cent and then ask your bank to defer the interest on your loan so that you don't fall behind on repayments.

4. **Refer to government legislation.** If the government has enacted legislation – such as a mandatory code of conduct covering how landlords and tenants are to deal with each other in the pandemic – all parties must comply with the legislation. This is designed to protect both the landlord, the tenant and the economy.

EPILOGUE

Commercial property is a great way to achieve your financial goals and achieving a passive income – it can enable you to live the happy life you desire without being tied down to a job! As you can see from the flowchart overleaf, there's quite a lot to know about it.

Whether you're a first-time or experienced commercial investor, I hope that this book has given you some extra knowledge and confidence with buying commercial property.

I wish you all the best in the future – happy investing!

'Success leaves clues. People who succeed at the highest level are not lucky; they're doing something differently than everyone else does.'

—Tony Robbins, *Money: Master the game*

The commercial property investing process - explained simply

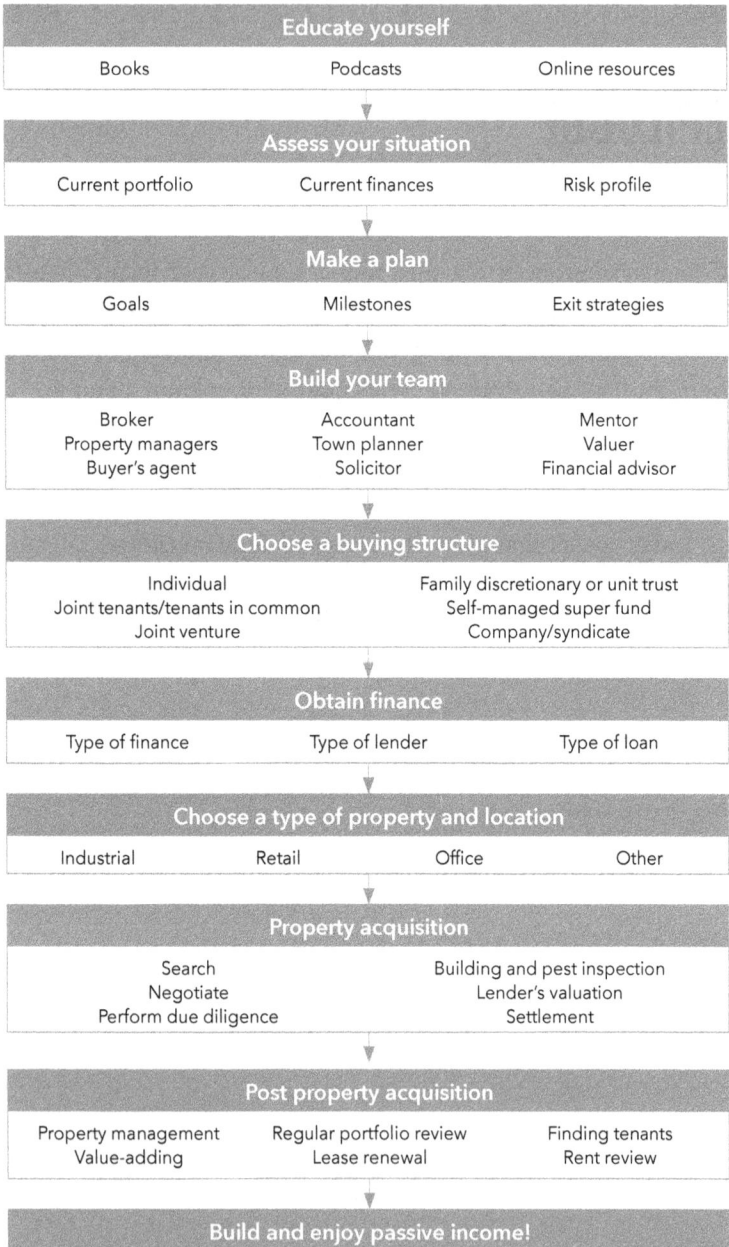

Educate yourself		
Books	Podcasts	Online resources

▼

Assess your situation		
Current portfolio	Current finances	Risk profile

▼

Make a plan		
Goals	Milestones	Exit strategies

▼

Build your team		
Broker	Accountant	Mentor
Property managers	Town planner	Valuer
Buyer's agent	Solicitor	Financial advisor

▼

Choose a buying structure	
Individual	Family discretionary or unit trust
Joint tenants/tenants in common	Self-managed super fund
Joint venture	Company/syndicate

▼

Obtain finance		
Type of finance	Type of lender	Type of loan

▼

Choose a type of property and location			
Industrial	Retail	Office	Other

▼

Property acquisition	
Search	Building and pest inspection
Negotiate	Lender's valuation
Perform due diligence	Settlement

▼

Post property acquisition		
Property management	Regular portfolio review	Finding tenants
Value-adding	Lease renewal	Rent review

▼

Build and enjoy passive income!

ABOUT THE AUTHOR

Steve Palise has worked for Australia's leading buyers' agencies, executing more than 1,200 property acquisitions and acquiring hundreds of commercial properties for himself and his clients. He has purchased in every capital city and all major regional towns in Australia.

In this book, and in his work, he draws on the mathematical and analytical skills developed in his previous life as a chartered mechanical and structural design engineer, to break down what works best in commercial property. As with engineering, commercial property investment is based primarily on the numbers.

Having acquired an impressive property portfolio that allowed him to leave the workforce sooner rather than later, he's now passionate about helping others to achieve their goals and financial freedom. His philosophy is that investments should increase your wealth and passive income with as little risk as possible.

Steve Palise is a licensed real estate agent experienced in sourcing quality commercial property investments. He has helped thousands of clients secure and purchase properties, and believes property investing should be not only smart, but enjoyable along the way!

CONSULTATION SERVICES

Steve Palise offers buyer's agent services in Australia for nationwide commercial property. Consultation is available for:

- Mentoring

- Portfolio review and strategy design

- Sourcing properties

- Conducting due diligence on a property

- Settlement process support

- Introduction to property managers, solicitors, insurers, etc.

- Tenant selection

To speak with Steve or to follow what he has been up to, please visit him online:

- **Website:** www.paliseproperty.com.au

- **LinkedIn:** www.linkedin.com/in/steve-palise/

- **Facebook:** www.facebook.com/commercialpropertyinvesting

ACKNOWLEDGEMENTS

There are plenty of people who helped bring this book to fruition, and I'm grateful to all of them. This book started as a short summary of key aspects of commercial property investing, but expanded into a book that would end up being published and in bookstores.

Thanks to everyone in the Major Street Publishing team who have helped me so much. Special thanks to Lesley Williams, the fun frontwoman; Vanessa Smith, editor extraordinaire; and the clever cover designer, Tess McCabe.

A special thanks to some of those closest to me, Lisa Hiscock and Ian Marsden. Your continued love and support whilst writing this book is very much appreciated. As discussed, from now on you may only refer to me as 'Steve Palise – published author'.

A big shout-out to the industry professionals who helped with review of the book. I really enjoy our unrestrained and entertaining professional relationship, I look forward to continuing our work together, and I cannot recommend your services enough! Thank you to Cameron Beattie (Diamond Finance), David Martell (Priority Legal Services), Kylie Bazzi (World Class Conveyancing), and Grant Simpson and Adam Leishman (The Commercial Guys).

Also, without the experiences of and support from my peers and colleagues I wouldn't have been able to write this book. You have all helped in some way throughout my career in property investing.

Thank you!

Steve Palise – published author

INDEX

value-adding 20, 128, 249-251
vendor finance 137, 145, 148,
    207-211
versatility 26, 28

wage growth 104
warehouse property 17, 25, 27
websites 129
weighted average lease expiry
    (WALE) 68-71, 201

Westfield 31
Womack, James 1
working from home 39

yield 12, 29, 47, 53-54, 87,
    136
– calculation 54, 71

zoning 163-164, 251